THE
South
ESTUARY

IT is a matter of some pride to me that I am able to pen the foreword to this Architectural Guide — hopefully the first of a series in the West of Scotland — published by the Royal Incorporation of Architects in Scotland. Like the adolescent, we are in the process of learning that our fathers were not wrong, and indeed, that we are the possessors of a heritage of outstanding quality. This reawakening of interest brings with it a new pride in our surroundings.

Dr Frank Walker — with a deep knowledge of his subject, a penetrating eye and a sympathetic understanding — brings to your attention many of the architectural gems which grace our Scottish Towns of Renfrewshire and the Clyde environs. When you read these pages, I hope you will be stimulated to go out and have a second — and more appreciative — look at the buildings, and develop a new understanding of the contribution our architectural forefathers have made to your environment.

DAVID J. LESLIE
PRESIDENT
The Glasgow Institute of Architects

Author: Frank Arneil Walker
Series Editor: Charles McKean
© *F. A. Walker and RIAS*

Scottish Academic Press
Royal Incorporation of Architects in Scotland
ISBN 7073 0476 8
1st edition 1986
Printed by Lindsay & Co. Ltd., Edinburgh

RCAHMS

The Districts of Renfrew and Inverclyde — the major part of what was once Renfrewshire — lie to the west of Glasgow, south of the Clyde's bend from estuary to firth. Around Glasgow the landscape is flat, stretching back from the ancient royal burgh of Renfrew to the edges of Paisley and on to Linwood Moss. Elsewhere, hilly country rolls across the valleys of the Levern, Black Cart, Calder and Gryffe to the high moorland of Loch Thom and Muirshiel Country Park in the west. From Langbank to Wemyss Bay, beneath steeply rising slopes and cliffs, the coastal margin is exceptionally narrow — a topography which, with its magnificent sunset-lit prospects across the firth to Argyll, adds a spectacular quality to the Tail-of-the-Bank townscape at Port Glasgow, Greenock and Gourock.

The routes along river valleys and riparian strip have always favoured rural settlement, but have had little or no strategic significance in Scotland's history. Few castles are to be found: a handful of crumbling tower houses only — though the Maxwell stronghold at Newark, Port Glasgow, is still splendid, despite its now compromised setting. There are some half dozen or so minor religious foundations whose antiquity reaches back to the first Christian millennium, but again only one great monastic house — Paisley Abbey.

On the other hand, the sudden enterprise of the late 18th century which transformed Scotland into an industrial nation found in these same river valleys a convenient and, given the legendary dampness of the west coast climate, a reliable source of power. Between

Paisley from the south, 1825. Aquatint by J. Clark.

Opposite Cloch lighthouse and the Tail of the Bank.

3

1780 and 1800, at least two dozen cotton mills had been built and soon, with the application of the rotative engine invented by James Watt, a Greenock man, steam power was introduced to the burgeoning textile industry. Factory villages sprang up at Barrhead, Gateside, Neilston, Linwood, Johnstone, Lochwinnoch, Crosslee, Houston and Bridge of Weir. Scarcely a rural community escaped while, at the heart of this social revolution, Paisley developed rapidly from a town of handloom weavers into a world centre of shawl manufacture and industrialised cotton spinning. Thread became the principal product providing the employment for a vast labour force and the patronage which has given the town most of its finest buildings.

Meanwhile, on the coast at Port Glasgow and Greenock, opportunities for Atlantic trade following the Union of 1707 had produced a thriving economy based on maritime commerce in sugar, rum, etc. with the West Indies and America. The related industries of rope-spinning and sail-making prospered and even *straw-hat manufacture has been prosecuted with much éclat*. But it was ship-building and latterly ironfounding and forging which for almost two and a half centuries were to be the economic backbone of both towns. As in Paisley, one industry dominated, though here the proletarian cast of the population was intensified first by the arrival of dispossessed Highlanders and later by destitute starving Irish. For many of these the Tail-of-the-Bank was little more than a staging-post *en route* to a new life in the New World; but many stayed on to find work in the shipyards and engine shops. To this day a religious divide is clear-cut and, though much less paralleled by socio-economic stratification, the cultures of the two communities remain in many ways distinct.

In Paisley the distinctly Protestant propensity for sectarianism ran unchecked. Here, the weavers — skilled men and, to some extent, economically independent; self-educated and articulate — *supported a culture of great interest*, as radical in politics as in religion. Sermons were dissected and discoursed upon with the fiercest theological commitment while *the arrival of the newspapers was a signal for work to stop until the leading articles had been discussed in the streets.* Christian conscience and political awareness coalesced in 1819-20 when unrest over industrial depression and growing unemployment culminated in riots and mass demonstrations. So popular was the cause that juries set up to convict captives taken in what was exaggeratedly referred to as the *Radical War* produced acquittals instead.

Radicalism in Paisley persisted through the denominationalism of Victorian religion (to which the

close-packed group of churches on Oakshaw Hill
testifies still) and into 20th century politics. With it
has gone a rather unusual cultural gloss — an
astonishing addiction to poetry-making. Rhyme and
rhythm may fly with the weaver's shuttle. At any rate,
as the writer of *A Short Account of the Town of Paisley*
noted in 1828, there seems to have been *among the
working classes . . . a degree of intelligence and a taste for
literature seldom met with. . . .*
Versifiers abounded, mostly of indifferent talent
aping the works of Burns or Scott. No more than a
few attained modest distinction: lyric poets like Robert
Tannahill and Gavin Turnbull, the satirist Alexander
Wilson who later became America's leading
ornithologist, and John Wilson, the Christopher North
of *Blackwood's Magazine.* Nonetheless, when Robert
Brown compiled his two-volume *Paisley Poets*
(1889-90) he felt able to include the works of more
than two hundred writers. One of those, John Kent,
deserves to be remembered if only for the brilliance of
his rhyme.

> *Yet Paisley's name is widely spread,*
> *An history doth show it's*
> *Been famed alike for shawls and thread,*
> *For poverty and poets.*

Organisation of this Book
This guide begins with Paisley, always the
principal town in Renfrewshire and still the centre
through which much of the rest of Renfrew District is
to be reached. Thereafter a series of river valley routes
is described: to the south-west the course of the upper
Levern from Barrhead to Neilston and on through the
Loch Libo gap to Uplawmoor and Caldwell; west
through Elderslie, Johnstone and Kilbarchan along the
Black Cart Water to Howwood and Castle Semple
Loch with Lochwinnoch beyond; north-west by
Linwood to Strathgryffe at Houston and Bridge of
Weir and into Inverclyde District at Kilmacolm.
Finally, from Renfrew the coastal route is followed via
Inchinnan, Erskine and Bishopton entering Inverclyde
at Langbank and continuing on through Port
Glasgow, Greenock, Gourock and Inverkip to reach
the pierhead terminus of Wemyss Bay.

Right of Access
Many of the buildings described in this guide are
either open to the public or are visible from the road.
As many are privately owned and not open to the
public, readers are respected to requested the occupiers'
privacy.

Liddell & White

Paisley Abbey and the Place of
Paisley from the west.

THE ABBEY

The foundation of **Paisley Abbey**, like all the great
religious houses of Scotland, has its French
connection. In 1163 Walter Fitz Alan, High Steward
of David I's kingdom, concluded an agreement with
the Abbot of Wenlock in Shropshire to build a
monastery at Paisley *according to the order of the
brethren of Wenlock, i.e. according to the order of the
monks of Clugny.* In little over a decade a priory had
arisen on the east bank of the White Cart close to the
site of the ancient chapel of the Celtic saint Mirin
and, by the middle of the 13th century, Clugny had
finally confirmed the papal bull of 1219 which gave
the monks at Paisley authority to elect their own
abbot. Of this early Abbey church some fragmentary
portions remain: a processional Norman doorway
(c. 1190) at the east end of the south aisle, three First
Pointed windows immediately west of this, and the
west doorway (early 13th century) with its blind
flanking arches not unlike Dunblane, also *in classic
lancet style.* Everything else is *restoration.*

The great aisled nave, Decorated Gothic
principally of the 15th century, was gradually
reconstructed after destruction by the English in 1307.
The aisles have sexpartite vaults and although the
nave is unvaulted it is distinguished by an arcaded
triforium of cusped tracery from the spandrels of
which massively corbelled projections pass around
alternate piers of a high clerestorey. The St Mirin
Aisle (1499), east of the south transept, has a pointed

barrel vault with decorative ribs. Crossing, choir and north transept, all restored during the 15th century, were largely destroyed in 1553 when the tower collapsed. Shortly after this the very theological fabric of the church split asunder and the Reformation ensured there would be no return to monastic forms, either liturgical or architectural. For more than three centuries the Abbey lay in ruins save for the nave, walled off as the parish kirk, and the south transept, serving for a time as a separate family chapel linked to the Place of Paisley (*q.v.*).

A plaster ceiling with painted vaulting was erected over the nave in 1788 (now replaced, 1980-81, by an open tied timber roof) but attempts at wholesale restoration had to await Victorian enthusiasms for ecclesiological *improvement.* Renovation of the nave and repairs to the transepts (1859-62) were begun by James Salmon and continued by R. Rowand Anderson who also started to raise the tower. Peter MacGregor Chalmers, architect to the Abbey until 1922, reconstructed part of the cloister and began to recreate the choir, incorporating a mediaeval piscina and unusual four-bay sedilia into the new walls. Finally, Robert Lorimer, with Alfred Lochhead, completed both the choir and the upper stage of the square tower. Lorimer's long vaulted choir is particularly precise and scholarly, his choir stalls impeccable. Yet — perhaps inevitably — the Abbey lacks a real sense of coherence between old and new, and the polished ashlar of its later work seems almost hypocritically studied beside the rude earnestness of the dark nave.

Paisley Museum

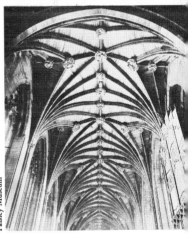

Paisley Museum

RCAHMS

Top Paisley Abbey west front; early 19th century.
Above Paisley Abbey; the nave showing triforium and corbelled clerestorey walk.
Left Paisley Abbey; the choir vault.

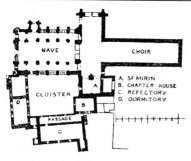

Plan of the Abbey and Place from MacGibbon and Ross, 1892.

The church contains many interesting monuments and tombs. Moved here from an exposed hilltop near Houston, the **Barochan Cross** (10th century?), a freestanding Celtic cross carved with interlaced ornament and figures in the manner of the so-called *Govan School*, can be found at the rear of the nave. Close by is Flaxman's memorial (1810) to William McDowall of Garthland; on the north side of the choir a recumbent female figure (late 13th century), reputedly the burial chest of Marjory, daughter of King Robert the Bruce; in the choir, too, the burial place of Robert III, marked by J. Hutchison (1888); and in the cloister court, a war memorial (1923), carried out by Jeffrey Waddell to a design of Reginald Blomfield.

South and east of the cloister court, abutting St Mirin's Chapel, are the black walls of the **Place of Paisley** (16th century). Originally closely associated with monastic life, the Place (or Palace) subsequently suffered various changes in ownership and condition — by the 19th century it had been indiscriminately flatted and even contained a public house — before its 20th century restoration. It comprises a four-storey-and-attic Scotch house, augmented on the south by a large L-plan addition (1675), two-storeys only, plain, but maintaining similar stylistic features — swept dormers, eaves dormers with gablet heads, crow steps and skews. The square pyramid-roofed tower (1961-62) is by local architect J. Steel Maitland who brought the Place back into church use, creating a manse out of part of the old fabric.

2 Clark Town Hall
W. G. Lynn (1879-82)
After several abortive proposals — two by James J. Lamb (1864, 1869) and one by Rennison and Scott (1875) — a competition design in free Classical idiom by the Belfast architect W. H. Lynn was finally built. Temple fronts — Corinthian on the east, Ionic to the north — articulate a high *piano nobile*. To the river the facade is more planar with a cantilevered balcony looking up to the centre of town. Above rise two towers, that to the north taller with clock, octagonal belfry and fishscale stone slated cap, while below channelled ashlar drops cliff-like to the river.

3 Municipal Buildings
Hutchison, Locke and Monk (1969-73)
Six storeys of high gritty grey offices, housing district and regional administration as well as police headquarters, stretch *en échelon* from the river to Gauze Street. The ribbed concrete is of unusually high quality, the construction detailing and landscaping excellent, but failure to complete two

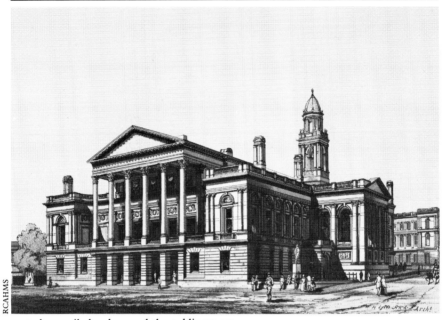

central council chambers and the public square between has left a vacuum of unresolved forms and untidy carparking at the heart of the composition. The addition of a single council suite (1984-85) on the east side of the development does little to help.

Secular and religious might seem fittingly concentrated around the graveyard sward which links Town Hall, Abbey and Council offices. There is no doubt that this is civic space — statues, green lawns, flower beds, and, best of all, a clutch of magnificent Cornish elms. But the void is too great, the buildings perhaps too monumental in their relationship. In fact, the real heart of the town is not here but just over the river unequivocally located at The Cross.

THE CROSS PLAN

Despite the likelihood that the oldest settlement at Paisley lay on the east bank on the White Cart *in the Seedhill*, close to the church founded by St Mirin in the 6th century and the mill that stood by an outcrop of rock in the river's course, the burgh's medieval expansion seems to have taken place almost entirely on the higher ground to the west.

Top George A. Clark Town Hall drawn by W. H. Lynn.
Above Municipal Buildings.

> *The bonnie toun o' Paisley,*
> *It stan's upon a hill,*
> *By it rins the River Cart,*
> *And ca's the Seedhill Mill.*

Blackhall before restoration as drawn by MacGibbon and Ross.

A view of central Paisley and the White Cart from Seedhill; 19th century.

4 **Blackhall Manor**
(from 16th century)
In the 12th century David I's High Steward had built a manor house across the river from the ancient village and some distance south of his Abbey. For centuries, however, it remained isolated as a hunting lodge. The present mansion (restored 1980-84) is based on a later construction.

Only in the 15th century does evidence of a small but thriving town on the west bank of the Cart begin to appear. While monastic inviolability prevails to the east, where the *Abby (sic) and Church, with its large orchards and gardens are enclosed with one of the most magnificent walls in Britain, all built with square stones upon both sides, about a mile in circuit,* plots across the river are being feued off for building land to sustain the hectic development of the young burgh. By 1489, a year after James IV had made Paisley a free burgh of barony, Moss Street (Mossgait), School Wynd (Bornyard), Stoney Brae (Common Passage), St Mirren Street (Water Wynd), Causeyside, High Street and Wellmeadow are all in existence. Half a millenium later these streets are still there. Their persistence confirms the deep-rootedness of Paisley's townscape, just as their almost exact directional coincidence with the cardinal points of the compass — Moss Street running north, High Street west, Causeyside south,

RCAHMS

and the Old Bridge leading east to the Abbey grounds — establishes a strong cross-based plan and divides the town into four major areas, each of which has had its own history of development giving spatial and social shape to its community.

Earliest growth was west from the bridge — *one principal street, well-built with handsome houses, about half a mile in length* which Crawfurd described in 1710. Parallel, along the ridge of Oakshawhead, ran another ancient lane from School Wynd to West Brae while, towards the end of the 18th century, further development in the West End was encouraged by the long straight line of George Street laid out to form another link between the centre of town and the new weaving villages of Maxwellton, built (c. 1746-50) as *the first place in Scotland where the silk trade began*, and *the cheerful appendage of Ferguslie* (begun 1777).

Growth to the south was also linear but more casual, with little expansion beyond the gushet of Neilston Road and Calside before the 19th century. Charleston (c. 1832) began as another weavers' suburb; with a reputation for particularly radical views, it was dubbed *the Republic*.

On the opposite side of town in the low-lying marshy ground at the foot of Moss Street (Moss Row) a grid iron plan was set down some time after the middle of the 18th century. This network of streets developed in rather imprecise alignments on each side of the river.

East of the river little existed besides a few houses clustered by the Abbey walls until, at the instigation of the Earl of Abercorn, who re-purchased the lordship of Paisley in 1764, the deer park and gardens of the Abbey were sold off. This became Paisley's New Town. Building began c. 1779, on new streets *laid off broad and straight, in a regular manner, but (rather unfortunately for the convenience and elegance of some of the houses) not in square angles*. Once again the impetus for development had come from an expanding weaving industry — as the street names testified: Lawn Street, Gauze Street, Silk Street, Cotton Street, Incle Street. Later, beyond the so-called New Town Cross which was situated at the junction of Gauze Street, Silk Street and Cotton Street, yet another weaving village was created at Williamsburgh (c. 1830), strung out along the road to Glasgow.

TOWN CENTRE

The Cross has always been both cross-roads and river crossing. **St James Bridge** (1883-84) is only the last in a succession of improvements (c. 1590, 1702-03, 1783, 1827) to the Old Bridge which, since the 15th century at least, spanned the White Cart, connecting

Paisley's growth during the second half of the 18th century was without parallel in Scotland. Between 1755 and 1821 its population increased almost sevenfold. Only Greenock, with a sixfold increase over the same period, approached this rate — though its total number of inhabitants remained half that of Paisley.

St James Bridge and the Clark Town Hall with former County Buildings in the back-ground; c. 1900.

Paisley Museum

County Buildings and Jail
(demolished) drawn by Joseph Swan.

Terrace Buildings

the Abbey to the converging routes of the town
centre. On the south side of the bridge the river
passes between the Town Hall and **Dunn Square**
(1894), a sloped formal garden, laid out by local
architect James Donald. A raised terrace curves
around Birnie Rhind's statues (1889) of two of
Paisley's greatest benefactors, Thomas and Sir Peter
Coats, before stepping down to James Shannon's
Dunn Fountain (1910), a bronze mother and child
group faintly charged with *Art Nouveau* eroticism.
The Square is united to the Town Hall by a common
Italianate mood carried across the bridge balustrade.
On the north side, however, disaster has struck:
between The Cross and **Abercorn Bridge** (1881,
widened 1910) at Old Sneddon, the river has vanished,
culverted below the so-called **Piazza** (1968-70), a
vastly vulgar development of shopping and offices.
For this open sore at the centre of the town the
castellated Gothic of William Reid's (or was it
Archibald Elliot's) County Buildings and Jail
(1818-20) had to be sacrificed; a strangely perverted
exchange indeed. Fortunately untouched, but
squeezed, are **Terrace Buildings** (1881) three storeys
of rich Italian Renaissance cake iced with a
balustraded eaves and swagged urns.
 Where the Jail stood, one arm of the Piazza's
pedestrianised precinct opens into **County Square**.

To the right is the ashlar viaduct of **Gilmour Street Station** (c. 1840 and later), the arched entrance to the booking hall flanked by octagonal turrets, castellated again, like its demolished neighbour, and Tudor too, like the red sandstone of W. W. Robertson's Board of Works **Post Office** (1892-93) which forms the west side of the Square with its higher Glasgow Style Baronial wing added by W. T. Oldgrieve in 1912. **1-5 County Place** (c. 1830), an uninterrupted three-storey tenement range, adds a classical component turning in quadrant corners back up Moss Street and Gilmour Street.

7   **1-7 Moss Street** (c. 1810) set an elegantly plain four-storey scale, continued in a cute octagonal turret at the corner of School Wynd. **10 Moss Street** (c. 1830), formerly the Assembly Rooms, is only two-storeys, but the eight bays on first floor are exceptionally tall. In Gilmour Street, Wilson Hamilton and Wilson have inserted a sleek little addition alongside James Salmon's **Bank of Scotland** (c. 1850), though they have brutalised the street level of both. Next door, the **Clydesdale Bank** (1910) by Craig Barr and Cook, is facade-thin Beaux-Arts, made to look a little meretricious by the disciplined skills of John Honeyman's Roman *palazzo* at **no. 9** (1876) or David Cousin's former British Linen Bank across the street at **nos. 4-6** (1866-68).

Where Moss Street and Gilmour Street begin there is generous space around Robert Lorimer's **War Memorial** (1922), its bronze equestrian statue, by A. Meredith Williams, looking down across The Cross
8 cross-roads. **Burton's** (1930) is the dominant corner; a high three-storeyed curve in white Art Deco classicism. But Honeyman's contribution at **10-12 High Street** (1871) — built into the site of the former Tolbooth (1757) after its steeple had finally to be demolished (1870) — is also good.

Paisley Museum

Strathclyde Region

Top Post Office, County Square, in the 1890s before its extension to the south.
Above The Cross, with Honeyman's 10-12 High Street on the corner and 1-7 Moss Street to the right.

Carson & Hunter

Burton's Corner, The Cross.

Paisley Central Library

Walker

Renfrew District

Top High Street, c. 1900.
Middle High Street; no. 30 to the left.
Above 7 Orr Square.

High Street, on the northern side, lives up to Honeyman's fine beginning. Woolworth's is a banal exception but otherwise **18-28** (c. 1880-83) have a consistent urban panache, a French Renaissance flavour clinging to their facades. Only at **30** (c. 1880) do the precise delineations of neo-Grec vary the formula, while at James Donald's **Liberal Club** (1886; altered by Peter Caldwell, 1901) this superb stretch ends in a second floor window arcade and a conical slated turret over the corner to Church Hill. The south side falls far short of this quality: George Boswell's Picture House (1912-13) now a **Mecca Social Club**, induces a precocious Art Deco out of miniaturised Beaux Arts (gilded interior even more so); **no. 35** (1933) is bravely but incongruously Modernist, cramped in an infill site; while T. G. Abercrombie's Beaux Arts **Y.M.C.A.** building (1908) is disappointing for one of Paisley's most inventive architects. From Church Hill to Orr Square the scale drops, the buildings are older, unremarkable and often dilapidated. **7-9 Orr Square** (early 19th century) is cool and reserved; two elegant Georgian mansions wisely set back above the bustle. **2-6 Storie Street** (1840), preserves a pilastered shopfront framed by a strongly dentilled fascia cornice. Above the curved sills and astragals of the **Bruce Arms** at 57-59 High Street (c. 1900) tenements begin, continuing to **63-69** (1898) where a four-storeyed red sandstone range splits symmetrically on either side of Townhead Terrace (1911).

Paisley Museum

Museum, Art Gallery and Library.

Paisley Shawls
Towards the end of the 18th century, Edinburgh and Norwich began to weave shawls with patterns based on Kashmir motifs. Around 1805 Paisley started production and within a generation it dominated the market. By mid century the teardrop or tadpole shapes were known all over the world as "Paisleys".

The earliest commercially manufactured examples were woven on a two-man drawloom but as this process constrained the flowing curves of the motif to a stepped outline it was Paisley's early adoption of the French Jacquard loom which made the difference. It required only one operative, was effective over a wider surface of the shawl and, most important, produced smooth curves. More efficiency, greater output and unscrupulous design piracy were the secrets of Paisley's success.

Paisley Museum preserves an example of a Jacquard loom together with a collection of over 700 shawls.

Paisley Shawls

11 Museum, Art Gallery and Library

John Honeyman (1868, 1881)

Steps lead up through a splendid portico of four finely cut Greek Ionic columns to enter what was at first a symmetrical building but was later successfully extended (1902) by Honeyman and Keppie using a similar but narrower temple front advancing on the east. The *stripped classicism* of a further wing (1933) by Keppie and Henderson, is less convincing. The museum's original galleried interior steps up the sloping site on a series of axial stairways to a coffered central cupola. For anyone seeking the story of the celebrated Paisley shawl, this is the place to be.

12 Territorial Army Centre

T. G. Abercrombie (1896)

Here at 76 High Street, Abercrombie is in more characteristic swaggering form than at the Y.M.C.A.; imaginative Scots Renaissance in polychrome sandstone, dormered and turretted, with an *Art Nouveau* bellcote.

A High Street bronze plaque recalls the "stately building with large garden and an imposing entrance", where John Wilson (1785-1854) — Christopher North of Blackwood's Magazine — once lived. A friend not only of Lockhart and Hogg, but of Wordsworth and Coleridge too, North is, with Tannahill, the best known of Paisley's prodigious population of poets. A bust by James Fillans — "I have sat to many, but I will never sit to another, the bust is so excellent", North told the sculptor — can be seen in the town's art gallery across the street.

Dept. of Environment

Territorial Army Centre.

Coats Memorial Baptist Church; illustrated in *The Building News,* 1897; the architect's R.S.A. Diploma Drawing.

13 **Coats Memorial Baptist Church**
Hippolyte J. Blanc (1894)
Still on the rising hillside of Oakshaw — more cathedral than kirk — a building of majestic form, its great crown spire tower dominating the line of High Street all the way from The Cross. Though its Early Decorated style is not unduly ambitious, its sheer size and setting are astounding. An immensely wide and high flight of steps rises to three gabled porches. Above are the five-light traceried windows and triple lancet of the south gable set between octagonal towers; behind, the church, cruciform in plan with gabled transepts and flying buttresses, sits on a huge undercroft of hall accommodation. It is Gothic Revival at its scenic best! Inside no expense has been spared, marbles and alabaster abound, the crossing and chancel have even been vaulted in stone: testimony as much to the munificence of the Coats family as to the ability of the architect.

Across the street is **Paisley College of Technology** (1962-63) seven floors of glazed-grid facade by Alison, Hutchison and Partners now much the better for the laboratories, workshops, etc. (1971-) with which Robert Matthew, Johnson-

Marshall and Partners have been filling the campus all the way to Abercrombie's original competition-winning building (1898) at 42 George Street. Downhill, beside the battered hulk of the old **Regal Cinema** (1932-34) by J. McKissack and Son, is Lady Lane, *one of the marches of the ancient burgh* and now the point at which the West End begins. At **17-25** (1891-92) — perhaps the finest tenements in town, an elaborately carved range by Peter Caldwell for the Paisley Provident Co-operative Society.

14

Walker

The road immediately south from The Cross was given its present form in 1872-77 when **St Mirren Street** was built up in a succession of gabled fronts by Baronial specialists, Peddie and Kinnear. Different in style from the north side of High Street, the same *variations on a theme* approach secures interest and consistency — though not without suffering some shopfitters' spoliation. Thereafter **Causeyside Street** begins as the preserve of the Co-operative Society: a stretch of tenements at **18-22** (early 19th century) given over to retailing; two infill blocks — one (1932) dominated by a colossal Beaux Arts aedicule at its centre, the other (1913) plainer and thus more *modern*; and at **25-29**, an ornate four-storey block (1907-08) by Robert Miller, rippling with shallow bays, almost Central European in its bulky exuberance. **13 Causeyside Street** (c. 1930) has a first floor articulated by rather Aztec pilasters between which sit Venetian windows and above which the reptilian ridge of a mansard snakes round into Forbes Place. **Forbes Place** (1835-38) itself runs down to the river in uniform ranges of warehousing built for the town's shawl manufacturers.

15

Walker

16 **Russell Institute**
J. Steel Maitland (1926-27)
On the corner with New Street two bronze and ashlar pyloned facades meet in a high glazed entrance made more symbolical than clinical by the sculpture of Archibald Dawson.

Laigh Kirk
James Baird and John Hart (1736-38, altered 1873)
Now an Arts Centre in an unexpectedly leafy enclave, this gabled T-plan kirk of crow-stepped lancets is the oldest church in the town other than the Abbey; crudely Gothic but robustly Scottish.
The **Unionist Club** (c. 1805), 26 New Street, is smoothly classical and eponymously British. W. D. McLennan's **Bull Inn** (1900-01), however, is again Scottish: a tall red tenement breaking the pattern of its neighbours with a free Baronial facade and Glasgow Style pub interior which contains some wonderful *Art*

17

MacLean

Top St Mirren Street.
Middle Buildings for the Co-operative Society, Causeyside Street.
Above Russell Institute.

B

Strathclyde Region

Laigh Kirk, now an Arts Centre.

Sma' Shot Cottages, 11-17 George Place, now the home of the Old Paisley Society, comprise a row of simple artisans' houses dating from the early and mid-19th century. The Society has restored their Victorian interiors naming one of the small exhibition rooms after Alexander Wilson (1766-1813), the Paisley weaver-poet who became the father of American ornithology.

Nouveau glass and joinery. Vestiges of the early 19th century streetscape survive: a good shopfront and pend at **12 New Street**, a weaver's house at **14 Shuttle Street** saved by the Old Paisley Society, a row of two-storey rubble cottages at **11-17 George Place**, now the Society's exhibition centre and tea-shop, and a grander five-bay symmetrical house with pedimented doorpiece and perron stair at **5 George Place.**

18 **St George's Church**
William Reid (1819, refurbished 1874)
A muscular mass fronted by four giant-order Ionic pilasters supporting a pediment with quadrant shoulders but without the octagonal steeple evidently intended. Interior recast by J. A. Rennison.

Carson & Hunter

St George's Church.

18

THE NORTH END

Everything beyond the Glasgow-Greenock railway
line, for which Parliamentary sanction was granted as
early as 1837, can be considered as Paisley's North
End. The raised track, cutting through the town as a
hefty viaduct of rock faced walls along Weir Street
and red sandstone ashlar down Old Sneddon, makes
an evident boundary. Sad to say, however, the gridded
network of streets which once gave a spatial coherence
from Caledonia Street on the west to Renfrew Road
on the east is now all but imperceptible, lost in a
wasteland of dereliction and road re-alignment.

19   **49-51 Moss Street** (early 19th century), a two-
storey house in droved ashlar with tripartite windows
and a fanlit corniced and architraved door, and **53
Moss Street** (early 19th century), three-storeys, with
Venetian windows and a dentilled eaves cornice, are
both beyond the bridge and formerly stood on St
James Place. So, too, did **Holy Trinity Church**
(1828, refurbished 1871), now islanded by traffic. It
still looks down the axis of **St James Street**, but its
pinnacled firescreen front is not up to it.

20 **Sheriff Court**
Clarke and Bell (1885)
A symmetrical two-storey *palazzo* with real presence,
projecting end bays are joined by a balconied Roman
Doric loggia. It was later almost outflanked by the
same architects' **County Buildings** (1890), now the
Procurator Fiscal's Office, which, inflecting to the

Sheriff Court and County
Buildings.

Dept. of Environment

St James Church.

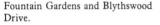

Fountain Gardens and Blythswood
Drive.

corner site, raise an off-centre Ionic temple on a
ground floor of channelled ashlar.

Beyond the skewed viaduct (1840) leading on to
Underwood Road lie Hippolyte Blanc's Gothic
21 Revival **St James Church** (1880, 1904), a cruciform
plan with double-gabled transepts and a high
asymmetrically placed steeple, and, by contrast
decidedly horizontal, the 39 glass and mosaic bays of
the **Milk Marketing Board Offices** (1967), by
Honeyman, Jack and Robertson.

Caledonia Street illustrates well the change in urban
scale which occurred over the course of last century.
At first, two- or sometimes three-storey flatted
housing: **5-7** plain and austere, except for their Roman
Doric doorways (the latter crudely proportioned); **11**
and **21** lower and older, preserving pedimented front
stacks. Finally, further north, more decorative four-
storeyed tenements, those forming a long fortress-like
block down **Blythswood Drive** and **Andrews Street**
rhythmically modelled by two-light centre mullion
bows. Beyond are more tenements lining the south
side of Greenock Road. Tucked up Greenhill Road,
just north of the motorway intersection, are the long
22 three-storeyed glazed walls of the old **Four Square
Factory** (1936-38), by J. Steel Maitland, its dado
stucco once as chic and white as the cigarettes it
produced.

Love Street parallels Caledonia Street. In the
23 **Fountain Gardens** (1868), sit four friendly cast iron
walruses protecting a multi-tiered fountain by the iron
founders G. Smith and Co. There are two-storeyed
ashlar houses (c. 1830) at **32, 34-36, 46-48** and **60.
50 Love Street** (c. 1830), more upmarket, is a small
late Georgian villa with an Ionic columned porch.
And again, at the north end of the street — tenements:
a surprisingly Thomsonesque door and window at
64, and a long powerful range (1904) running from

the Gardens to Albion Street. **4 Glen Street** (1899) is
an isolated maverick; a quirky imaginative inter-
pretation in four-storeyed red sandstone by W. D.
McLennan.

24 **Nethercommon Carpet Works**
T. G. Abercrombie (1912)
Bright brick polychromy, after the fashion set by
Templeton's in Glasgow, leads into Inchinnan Road.
The facade design has twelve of its sixteen bays
corbelled out at second floor on segmental arches
spanning between broad piers. By coincidence (surely)
these arches turn out to be something of a prelude for
Glasgow Airport half a mile down the road to the
north.

25 **Glasgow Airport Terminal Building**
Sir Basil Spence, Glover & Ferguson (1963-66)
Sixteen bays have segmental arches forming a long,
panelled fascia above glazed walls. The shape is a
Spence stereotype by now (Sussex University *et al.*)
but there is a flightiness about it that lifts the all-too-
easily dispirited traveller above the shuttling efficiency
of such places. Unfortunately the same cannot quite
be said for the ten internationally packaged storeys of
the **Excelsior Hotel** (1970-71).

26   **Adelphi House** (c. 1800), 91-93 New Sneddon
Street, is a pavilion-roofed Georgian mansion with a
porch of coupled Ionic columns but considerably
demeaned by its squalid environment. **Beauchamp
House,** 38-40 New Sneddon Street (c. 1775), grander

27 still, has a 5-bay front with a portholed pediment and
eaves cornice, architraved and corniced windows and a
pedimented door flanked by Corinthian half columns:
it exists only as an empty shell waiting for a better
future. At **20-22 Back Sneddon Street** (1898), T. G.
Abercrombie, in Scots Renaissance idiom, has devised
an irregular T-plan building full of inventive formal
combinations agitated by variations in the colour and
dressing of the sandstone.

Top 4 Glen Street.
Above Glasgow Airport.

Beauchamp House as shown on
Semple's Map of 1781.

The story *of the Chivas commission is an unusual one. No repetition of their bronzed glass skyscraper in New York for the whisky giant's Scottish outpost. Instead "The Building was to look as if it had been built in 1801 when two Aberdeenshire grocers, the Chivas Brothers, had first marketed their whisky". In the event, the anachronism was more extreme. After the late 17th century model of Caroline Park at Granton, near Edinburgh, had met with US approval, the architects evolved their final design from six submitted alternatives. What had begun "with grave misgivings" ended in determination "to make it the best modern Scottish old house and as authentic as we could get it."*

Boys Jarvis

Right Chivas Building.
Below Wallneuk Church.
Bottom Trident House.

MacLean

Hutchison, Locke, Monk

28 **Wallneuk Church**
T. G. Abercrombie (1913-15)
Across the river on Abercorn Street Abercrombie turns to Perpendicular Gothic to create one of his best works. Here the asymmetrical composition is calmer, rising gradually to its climax in an exquisite buttressed and battlemented belfry.

The destruction of the North End is pervasive: only to the north along **Renfrew Road** does any satisfactory relationship between buildings and street revive. From **86-88 to 100** a row of early 19th century houses re-establishes *rapport*; most date from c. 1820 but the low scale, small windows and narrow central door of **96-98** suggest it may be older — it is certainly archetypal architecture committed to the primitive power of solid over void. Infinitely more sophisticated is John Honeyman's Italianate **Monkshaw** (1871), confusingly re-named Sandyford House, at 121 Renfrew Road. This west side of the road has a handful of Victorian villas but it is not predominantly residential. **Abercorn School** (1902) by James Hutchison is tall School Board symmetry in rough red sandstone, rescued from orthodoxy by bold *Art*
29 *Nouveau* parapets in the wings. The **Chivas Building** (1962-64) by Lothian Barclay, Jarvis and Boys is sham Scots: a little French, a little William Adam, and a little ill at ease in its proportions. Nonetheless, something of a *tour de force* — as are the corrugated concrete catenary roofs of the bonded warehouses
30 behind. At the slip road to the M8, **Trident House** (1974-75) by Hutchison, Locke and Monk, a sombre Y-plan office block in precise brown brick, broods darkly behind its trees.

OAKSHAW

There is a persistent local tradition that a Roman *castellum* was sited at Oakshawhead. It is easy to see why. A steeply flanked ridge runs east-west commanding a secure outlook over the surrounding countryside. Chalmers in *Caledonia* says *No one has ever denied to Paisley the honour of a Roman station*, yet there is no conclusive evidence of a permanent Roman presence and none of serious fortification then or later. But when Paisley began its development in the 15th century it was natural that the town would soon spread uphill from The Cross. Today this mediaeval pattern is still clear in the narrow lanes and vennels climbing to the slow hilltop curve of Oakshaw Street.

The buildings, of course, are later: gable-to-gable housing fronting the narrow run-rig feus that stretch down to High Street on the south; some early 19th century villas on the north side of the hill where the feus are later and larger; and a concentration of churches gathered together in spikey silhouette — a fortress of faith above the town.

Religious sectarianism has its stylistic reflection. **St John's Church** (1862-63) by James Salmon and Son, is a tall galleried nave in polychromatic Second Pointed Gothic; towerless but with high pinnacled buttresses pierced by quatrefoils. The **Congregational Church** (1887, hall 1894) is also polychromatic but First Pointed; it has a graceful steeple rising from a square tower through diagonal buttresses to an octagonal spire. **Oakshaw East U.F. Church** (1826), now auction rooms, adopts (*pace* Ruskin) a pagan temple model; all in the severe manner of John Baird I. Even more austere is the old **Gaelic Church** (1793) at 20 Oakshaw Street, a piend-roofed rubble box kirk with alterations (1909) by T. G. Abercrombie which do little to relax the lingering rigour of meeting-house religion. But on Church Hill there are two fine examples of that union of classicism and Reformed religion which characterises the best of 18th century Scots kirks.

Top High Church from Church Hill.
Above Congregational Church with the steeple of the High Kirk beyond.

32 **The High Church**
John White (1750-56)
The steeple (1770) rises in five stages to its obelisk spire — Venetian window motifs incorporated above the main arched entrance and in the balustraded fourth stage. The broad galleried church is pavilion-roofed with round-headed windows and oculi, and an excellent doorpiece on the north in good English Baroque. John White, a local baillie, also built the town's Tolbooth. Rennison and Scott later renovated the interior (1876-77).

Orr Street.

Thomas Graham Abercrombie (1862-1926) was certainly Paisley's most prolific architect. After training with the Glasgow architect John Hutchison, to whom C. R. Mackintosh was later apprenticed, and spending a few years in America, he established a practice in the town's High Street. By the 1890s he was at work on some of Paisley's largest buildings — notably the Royal Alexandra Infirmary (q.v.) and the Territorial Army Drill Hall (q.v.) — combining Scots Baronial and Scots Renaissance elements in a creative free style idiom. Over the next three decades the workload was immense: public buildings, tenements, churches, large private houses; scarcely a street in the town remained untouched.

In 1921, James Steel Maitland (1887-1982) became Abercrombie's partner. Maitland continued the practice until 1963, adding a dash of more Modernist flavour to the Scottish eclecticism he inherited.

Renfrew District

33 Middle Church
(1779-81)
Although there is no tower the west elevation has considerable elegance: squared rubble with ashlar dressings and in-and-out quoins, and a pedimented porch. In 1884 John Hutchison recast the interior completely, reorientating the internal layout at right angles to the main entrance. Further alterations since 1981 have continued the inner destruction.

The **Middle Church Halls** (1895-96), on the corner of School Wynd, are in well-detailed Renaissance by the ubiquitous Abercrombie. Further west **Orr Square Church** (1845) varies the skyline with Romanesque Revival. The former **Cameronian Church** (1810-11) at 62-64 Oakshaw Street, reverts to a rubble box, unrecognisably devotional after a recent conversion to flats. But across the street there is total assurance — religious and architectural — in Coats Memorial Baptist Church (q.v.), a splendid climax to this clutch of hilltop churches.

Religion gives Oakshaw its picturesque accents but housing gives it cohesion — especially along the spine of **Oakshaw Street**. 35 (early 19th century) is a flat two-storeyed gabled house with Roman Doric door;

Right Coats Observatory and Oakshaw Street looking west.

RCAHMS

Oakshaw Street houses.

51-55 are similar with three dormers and aberrant Greek Doric pilasters flanking a high doorway. Tenements increase the scale but do not destroy the continuity. Neither does Honeyman's **Coats Observatory** (1883) beautifully executed in channelled and polished ashlar with a great Doric frieze and cornice supporting a balustrade around the observation drum; nor does McKay and Forrester's infill villa at **33 Oakshaw Street** (1966) cleverly turning the corner into the walled defile of Orr Street. Several detached villas (c. 1820-30) step down the northern slope, accessible from Oakshaw Street but most with porches at the lower garden level. **60 Oakshaw Street**, has a roofless Gothic pavilion in the garden. **66-68** (1810), the former manse of the Cameronian Kirk next door, rubble-built with ashlar margins, has a *Gothic cornice* over its central door. Further on, stepping down the hill to Wellmeadow, **1-7 West Brae** (c. 1800) recall the humbler streetscape of the 18th century town.

Churches, houses — and schools. J. and J. Lamb's **Oakshaw School** (1863, extended 1888 by Charles Davidson) makes a tough Tudor facade when seen from School Wynd below, but is now only a screen to the gap left by demolishers. Rehabilitation is desperately needed here and at the old **Grammar School** (1802). This two-storey and attic gabled building on Church Hill, planned by Robert Barr, has its entrance on the Oakshaw side set below a projecting rubble turnpike.

34

Former Grammar School.

West Brae looking up to the John
Neilson Institution.

Renfrew District

35 **John Neilson Institution**
Charles Wilson (1849-52)

Founded by endowment in the 1840s, the school was
built on the elevated site at Oakshawhead which had
long been used as a bowling green and where,
according to Knox's survey of 1829 (although not
Semple's in 1781) there were *remains of a Roman
castellum or pretorium.* Wilson's plan is cruciform with
high classrooms disposed around a central octagonal
hall. From this massive parapetted bulk a *porridge bowl*
cupola emerges, the profile judiciously enlivened by
four decorative tripods carrying vases. More
Neoclassical than Italianate, it is perhaps Wilson's
finest work, its contribution to the skyline of Paisley
every bit as valuable as his Trinity College towers are
to Glasgow's Park hill. Like Trinity College it needs a
new use urgently. Empty, bricked up and vandalised,
it is a reproachful monument to indifference.

Meeting House Lane which leads
from Moss Street up into Oakshaw.

Renfrew District

Reproach indeed is the word that comes to mind
after a walk through Oakshaw. This should be the
most delightful part of town; topographically,
architecturally, it is splendid. But almost everywhere
there is cause for shame, from the failure to capitalise
on such an incomparable asset as the Neilson School
to the *graffiti* and detritus that scar the streets. One
need only look at what has happened to the
marvellous legacy of slivered whin paving, setts and
cobbles to wonder if anyone in Paisley really cares.

THE WEST END

Most Scottish towns have a salubrious West End. Not
so Paisley where, during the thread boom of Victorian
times, the weaving villages of Maxwellton and
Ferguslie fused into one extended proletarian suburb
stretching from the mills at Ferguslie to the centre of
town. Of the earlier weaving town streetscape not
much can be found: nothing along George Street and
Canal Street — cleared during the 1950s and '60s to
make way for new housing which included the town's
first high rise block — and further west, only a few
isolated relics. Some low-scale dwellings leading into
Sandholes Street; a symmetrical rubble-built house
with a slender central chimney at **57 Maxwellton
Street**; a similar unit at **15-19 Ferguslie Walk**
retaining its facade pediment — though not its
chimney: all these must date from the early decades of
the 19th century if not earlier. And there is, too, **11
Queen Street** (1755), a rubble cottage still thatched
at the front; preserved because it was the home of the
poet Robert Tannahill (1774-1810).

Looking east from Broomlands
Street into Wellmeadow; Oakshaw
and the John Neilson Institution to
the right.

Walker

*Time has been less kind to
Tannahill himself. No doubt his
work was, as one recent critic put it,
"a pale and sentimental imitation of
Burns's songs" and no doubt, like
Burns, he suffered by the eclipse of
Lallans Scots. But Tannahill's
tragedy was that he experienced this
rejection during his own lifetime and
could find neither the talent nor the
will to overcome it. When a revised
edition of his poems was returned
unread it was too much: he fell into
depression, destroyed all the
manuscripts he could find, and
finally drowned himself in the
Candren Burn not far from his home
in Queen Street. Rejected in love ten
years before, he had perhaps already
anticipated a maudlin epitaph.*

*"Noo the plantin taps are ting'd
   wi goud,
on yon burn side,
And gloamin draws her fuggy
   shroud
o'er yon burn side,
Far frae the noisy scene,
I'll thro the fiel's alane,
There we'll meet — My ain dear
   Jean!
doun by yon burn side."*

Paisley Central Library

During the 19th century, tenement flats, housing a
growing population of millworkers, replaced the
weavers' cottages. **Wellmeadow** shows the effect of
this change but is confused and run-down. **Walker
Street** and **Argyle Street** are better — though more
for their uniformity than quality. **Well Street**, too, is
straightforward but good — all the better for a recent
face-lift and the integration of new residential building
to the west and east, although of the new housing here
only Robert Matthew and Johnson-Marshall's
Student Residences (1980-85), climbing up Oakshaw
Hill, make an effort to come to terms with the scale
and colour of the tenements.

Beyond the top of Well Street there is a tall
tenement at **38 Wellmeadow** (1899) in an off-beat
classical mode so attenuated as to be almost *Art
Nouveau*. **4 Sandholes Street** (1880) is also special;
this time neo-Grec, with the influence of Thomson
evident in pilastered windows, friezes and ironwork.
The gushet of **West End Cross** (1886) is detailed in
orthodox classical style but distinguished by a
symmetrical corner composition with quadrants and,
above, a slated pyramid supporting a clock tower. **8-10
Broomlands Street** have shopfronts in cast iron with
the same cast iron columns repeated as freestanding
mullions to the tripartite windows above. **7-9 King
Street** (c. 1900) sets three storeys of flats above the
elliptically arched arcade of a pub. Only further west
on **Maxwellton Road** (once the Main Street of the
village) is there some reversion to lower scale: **69-83**
(c. 1886) continue the feel of a narrow survivor at
85-87 (c. 1820) to form a long terrace range with
scrolled stacks in front and stone gables at the rear.

Top West End Cross in the late
19th century.
Below Tannahill's Cottage in
Queen Street.

37

38

RCAHMS

Paisley Museum

39 Ferguslie Mills
James Coats built his first threadmaking factory at
Ferguslie in 1826 and, although there were then many
firms competing in the field, within half a century two
families — Coats and Clark — dominated the industry.
Amalgamating in 1896 with firms in Meltham and
Bolton, they became the world's leading manufacturers
of cotton sewing thread. During the 1880s Coats
expanded at Ferguslie, engaging the Bradford
architects Woodhouse and Morley to design what have
justly been called *the most magnificent cotton mills in
Scotland*. A hundred years on, most of the buildings
have gone. **No. 1 Spinning Mill** (1887) still stands —
an immense five-storeys of cast-iron and concrete
fireproof construction clad in red brick with ashlar
dressings, a balustraded and gabled eaves and copper-
clad turrets. Derelict and abandoned, there is still a
capitalist grandeur about it — as there is in the huge
cast iron fanlight of the **North Gatehouse** (c. 1890).

In the manner of enlightened paternalism, Coats'
interest in their thousands of employees was not
confined to the shop floor. No doubt the concern for
welfare was not disinterested but it certainly improved
the working lot of several generations of West Enders.
The **Mill Dining Hall** (1884), now a burnt-out shell,
was a grand affair in gabled Scots Renaissance.

40 Ferguslie School (1887), known locally as the Half-
Timers' School, was built in Woodhouse and Morley's
most ornate brick and ashlar Renaissance, absurdly
flamboyant even for the night-club it has become.
Abercrombie's **Girls' Club and Hostel** (1899) at 27
Ferguslie had a balconied and pedimented Mannerist
frontispiece.

Paisley Central Library

Renfrew District

Top Ferguslie Mills at the height
of production.
Middle No. 1 Spinning Mill,
Ferguslie.
Above West Gatehouse, Ferguslie
Mills.

Top Martyrs' Church.
Above Castlehead Church.

As for churches, even Coats could not make Baptists of their entire workforce. There was indeed a plethora of Baptist churches — **George Street** (1844), and **Lady Lane** (1867), both conventional buttressed gable fronts; **Walker Street** (c. 1900) an unorthodox octagon; and, culminating the family's philanthropy, the spectacular Coats Memorial (*q.v.*). But there were
41 alternatives. **Martyrs' Church** (1835), a high hall kirk with slender lancets, built by Barr and Lighton for *friends of the Church of Scotland*, sits at the entrance to Woodside Cemetery (laid out 1845;
42 **Crematorium**, 1937-38, in stucco and ashlar Moderne by J. Steel Maitland). **Martyrs' Memorial** (1847) is a smaller post-Disruption kirk with a facade and dumpy corner tower in neo-Norman added by Abercrombie (1904-05). **St Mary's Church** (1891) on George Street, is straightforward nave-and-aisles Pugin and Pugin Decorated.

43 **Castlehead Church**
(1781-82, refurbished 1868)
Originally the West Relief, another tall hall, *substantial, sombre and stark*, it sits at the foot of a wooded graveyard which contains Tannahill's tomb (1810) and those of several victims of the 1832 cholera epidemic.

South of Canal Street, drenched in greenery, the residential suburb of Castlehead is in every way the obverse of Ferguslie Park on the opposite north side of this end of town. Separated by the West End proper, each lies across its railway line *on the other side of the tracks*: one, a leafy, hilly enclave of private villas; the other, a bleak flat ghetto of council scheme houses. Castlehead is mid- to late-Victorian. Garden walls and gate posts define the street line, but the villas themselves vary the permutation of porches (note the beautiful fanlit doorway at **5 Main Road**), gables, bows and bays. There is, of course, the exception: noticeably black and white amid all the
44 sandstone is **The Old House** at 14 Main Road, a late 18th century house now roughcast but preserving its quoins, skews and string courses.

William Daniel McLennan
(1872-1940), son of a local shawl manufacturer and educated at the town's John Neilson Institution, set up practice in Paisley High Street late in 1895 or early in 1896. From the outset a predilection for half-timbered Tudor in both residential and commercial projects was infected by the attenuated decorativism of Glasgow Style Art Nouveau. It is unlikely that he was a member of Mackintosh's circle but certainly knew the work of his Glasgow contemporaries. McLennan's idiom was more robust and vigorous, cruder perhaps, but uniquely personal; at its best in The Bull Inn (q.v.) and St Matthew's Church (q.v.). By the time of the First World War his notepaper and drawings began to carry the heading "Architect and Civil Engineer", an index not only of the kind of commissions he was receiving but also of a willingness to experiment more with modern materials, methods and forms, e.g. at Crosslee Mill (q.v.). Never quite coming to terms with the Modernism of the 20s and 30s, he remainined something of a mysterious and cranky outsider.

Left St Matthew's Church, formerly St George's U.F. Church, showing original intention for unbuilt steeple.

THE SOUTH END

Three routes lead out through the south side of the town. The first crosses the river south of the Abbey at the cast-iron **Abercorn Bridge** (1763, widened 1829, rebuilt 1879-81) and continues from Orchard Square into Lonend and then, as the A726, through Blackhall south eastwards in the direction of East Kilbride. The second, the B774, follows Causeyside Street and Neilston Road to Barrhead. The third climbs up from Calside to Stanely and, as the B775, heads over Gleniffer Braes towards Caldwell, Lugton and Irvine.

St Matthew's Church from the east.

Orchard Square belies its name — doubly: no Abbey orchards, of course, but no real square either — simply an open swathe of traffic routes and car parking. There is, however, one building not only of local but national importance.

45 **St Matthew's Church**
W. D. McLennan (1905-07)
Formerly St George's U.F., this is perhaps Scotland's

Renfrew District

Paisley Museum

Strathclyde Region

Top Ardgowan Hotel, formerly Silver Thread Hotel.
Middle Causeyside Street tenements.
Above 96 Causeyside Street.

most *Art Nouveau* church. Inside and out, McLennan's design is tough, a little graceless, but never effete. What begins as neo-Perpendicular Gothic ends in a Glasgow Style idiom both expressionist and constructivist (*vide* the furnishings and roof trusses of the interior). Had the massive belfry spire been built it would have outscaled any other piece of *Art Nouveau* architecture in the country.

Rhetoric is not the touchstone of the **Watermill Hotel**; in 1968 the rubble walls of an old mill facing Clark's Anchor Mills (*q.v.*) across the river were saved and quietly converted by T. M. Miller and Partners. Much more aggressive are the orange brick and concrete frame of **Ardgowan Hotel** (1964) by James Cunningham and Partners. Situated on the acute junction with Blackhall Street it follows a butterfly plan of sorts with a serrated cornice storey of cantilevered bedroom bays.

Over the railway the crow-stepped gable of Blackhall manor (*q.v.*) appears through trees on the left. To the right are the secluded feus of some pleasant late Victorian villas on Hunterhill.
46 **Hunterhill House** (1902-03), Ardgowan Avenue, is best; in fact Edwardian in date, and also in style — T. G. Abercrombie in stone-and-harl Arts and Crafts mood. Back downhill the Barrhead Road continues through suburban public and private housing until it reaches green fields.

Causeyside Street running south from The Cross has some of the best tenements in town. It is not without older remnants — dilapidated properties between New Street and George Street include a good Roman Doric doorpiece with concave reveals at **48**, and an older pedimented tenement at **60** — but four-storey facades are the rule. **33** (1905-06) by T. G. Abercrombie turns into Orchard Street with a Baronial cap-house; **47-49** (1903), again Abercrombie, prefers a pagoda roof corner to Johnston Street; **51** (1902) is red Baronial; **78** (1903) has its top storey decorated with strapwork, each of its canted bays topped in an ogee cap and a turret over the corner bow; **87-89** are, by contrast, plain ashlar with only architraves and cornices for relief; **96** (1905) is a symmetrical composition climaxing in a gable stack arched down to a balcony at second floor level. Almost the only intrusion on these residential street walls is **St**
47 **Andrew's Church** (c. 1850); lancets and bellcote to the front, triforium-like arcading half-way up the transept gables.
48 A Tempietto **Fountain** (c. 1900) in pink granite marks the gushet at the start of Neilston Road. To the left is **Espedair Street**: at **15-19** (early 19th century), three gable-to-gable weavers' (?) houses each with its chimneyed pediment (**15** has marriage initials and a

date of 1835); at **31-35** a Thomsonesque block with
stepped architrave moulding, stub column capitals and
Greek fret. **Neilston Road** continues with tenements.
8-18 (c. 1870) are ashlar, uniform in elevation except
for an unusual variation of the ground floor flat
49 doorways. **57-61 Neilston Road** and **48-54 Stock
Street** (c. 1885), bayed in two-light windows, meet
below a raised square clock tower (1887) which is
brightly painted and has a flat-topped ogee *dome*. **65
Neilston Road** (c. 1890) has a central scrolled
chimney stack, Greek frets cut at first and second
floors, and a single shopfront surviving in original
form. James Lamb's **St Luke's Church** (1836,
additions and alterations in 1891 by James Donald) is
50 a plain lancetted gable. The **South School** is equally
plain but round-arched — one of the four early School
Board buildings designed by local architect and poet
William Stewart, *a gifted votary of the Muses*! Later
additions (1893-95) by T. L. Watson, full of
curvilinear gabling, are another matter altogether, and
further along Neilston Road the exhilarating red roof
of a third **South Primary School** (1985), by
Strathclyde Region Architects, yet another.

51 **Royal Alexandra Infirmary**
T. G. Abercrombie (1896-1900)
Scots Renaissance — or Baronial — or *Art Nouveau*:
the inventive exuberance of Abercrombie's design is
impossible to pidgeon-hole. From a bartizaned water-
tower keep the ward wings stretch out in E-plan to
end in semi-circular verandahs. Piended roofs are
pepper-potted with ventilators, the most splendid of
which sits on the ridge of the former dispensary block,
crowned by an *Art Nouveau* weather vane flourish.

99 Neilston Road (c. 1830), recalling the village
streetscape of Charleston, is a two-storey ashlar house
with familiar central pediment and chimney. But later
tenements soon return to define the street as far as
Braids Road. Up to the right, overlooking Brodie
52 Park, there are more; at the junction of **Carriagehill
Drive** and **Brodie Park Avenue** a particularly good
double-drummed corner.

Paisley Central Library

Tenement tower at corner of
Neilston Road and Stock Street.

Strathclyde Region

Tenements at Carriagehill
Drive/Brodie Park Avenue.

C

Top Little Croft, Southfield Avenue.
Middle Crosbie, Moredun Road.
Above Upton, Corsebar Road.

Farther south on **Falside** is T. G. Abercrombie's row of flatted *villas* (1911-13) built by Brown and Polson Ltd. to house their employees. Each has a wide twin-gabled elevation with half-timbering and bargeboards dipping low at each end of the facade. On the east side of Neilston Road is the suburb of Thornly Park; three parallel roads of bourgeois villa-land. Of the original Edwardian houses those by W. D. McLennan at **10, 12** and **31 Thornly Park Avenue** (1899-1905) are outstanding; all in white roughcast with red tiles and woodwork, unorthodox in form, idiosyncratic in detail — Tudorised *Art Nouveau*. McLennan's last major house **Thorscrag** (1924-27) is not far off on Barbourhill half-way to Barrhead. What seems from a distance to be a red sandstone mansion in a somewhat Elizabethan mould reveals itself on closer inspection as concrete-framed Tudorised *Art Deco*! More thoroughly committed to the transition from Arts and Crafts to modernism is J. Steel Maitland's **Little Croft** (1924-36), 21 Southfield Avenue.

A third route south starts in Calside. First there is some older housing — a terrace row at **5-19** (c. 1850), a rubble cottage at **43** (c. 1830) and, at the corner of Alice Street, **Rosebank** (early 19th century) a late Georgian town house. But once uphill feus are more spacious and houses grander. **Sanctuary** (1891-92), formerly Roneil, on Stanely Road, is an Arts and Crafts L-plan by T. G. Abercrombie rambling in cosy complexities; to the west is an octagonal conservatory on a stone plinth and to the east a particularly lovely tile-hung bedroom gable. William Leiper's **Moredun House** (1890) is in rather intimidating Jacobean, but its pyramid-roofed **Lodge** (1900) has Arts and Crafts charm. **Whiteleigh** (c. 1896) is a red and white villa by Abercrombie rising irregularly to three storeys. **Newark House** (c. 1890?) is big red Baronial with cable moulding, strapwork and thistles around the entrance. Grandest of all is **Crosbie** (1901-02), Abercrombie's domestic masterpiece, a vast L-plan mansion drawing English and Scottish forms into its free-wheeling Arts and Crafts composition. More unique, is **Upton** (1935-36), at 141 Corsebar Road, a house of a different generation but very much a period piece — white-walled Moderne with an Art Deco door framed in a single bold arch; the hand of Basil Spence?

RCAHMS

Renfrew District

Swan

53

54

55

56

57

Baxter, Clark, Paul

58   **Paisley District General Hospital** by Baxter,
Clark and Paul spreads out above Meikleriggs trim
and efficient in blue brick, but a rather sterile
exchange for Abercrombie's Royal Alexandra
Infirmary (*q.v.*). Otherwise this south-west side of
Paisley is endless residential suburbia. The huge
housing scheme mazes of Glenburn and Foxbar have
all but concealed the braes of Gleniffer that the young
Christopher North looked out on from Townhead and
Tannahill wandered across in love-sick reverie.

Paisley District General Hospital.

> *Keen blaws the win o'er the braes o' Gleniffer,*
> *The auld castle's turrets are covered wi snaw;*
> *How changed frae the time when I met wi my lover*
> *Amang the brume bushes by Stanely green shaw;*

59 **Stanely Castle**
The *auld castle's turrets*, i.e. its corbelled bartizans,
have fallen but the structure itself still stands to the
wallhead. Built in the 15th century by the Maxwells
of Newark, the L-plan structure has been saved by its
site in Stanely Reservoir, but further west, **Lounsdale
House** (1788), may be less fortunate.

Stanely Castle.

Paisley Museum

35

Carson & Hunter

Paisley Museum

Renfrew District

Top Gauze Street; Methodist Central Halls and Arnott's.
Middle Abercorn Inn, as shown on Semple's map of 1781.
Above Gauze Street; early 19th century houses and Clydesdale Bank infill.

THE EAST END

When the Earl of Abercorn built his New Town in the last quarter of the 18th century, he was careful to ensure that only grand and elegant houses should be erected. He himself had a large bow-fronted **Inn** (1780-83) constructed at the New Town Cross, i.e. at the saltire crossing of Gauze Street and Silk Street, to a design by George Stewart, *Architect at London*. The inn has gone — and with it the entire street layout south of Gauze Street — but a handful of early houses

60 at **23-31 Gauze Street** (c. 1780-85) remain to evoke the Classical streetscape Paisley enjoyed before economic pressures transformed it into what one mid-Victorian writer called *a singular alteration of handsome with mean edifices*.

The same description could apply today. Watson and Salmond's facades of Renaissance invention at the

61 **Methodist Central Halls** (1908), on the corner of Smithhills, and the canted bays of bronze-framed windows which J. Steel Maitland produced for Cochran's (1927), now **Arnott's**, opposite the Abbey, make handsome enough facades. Even the garishly red brick bays which Hutchison, Locke and Monk have strung around the corner of Lawn Street at **Refuge Assurance House** (1977-79) have formal conviction. So, too, does their rough and smooth concrete

62 **Clydesdale Bank Building** (1969-70), on Gauze Street, sensibly designed as infill and to cope with a wide lateral exposure resulting from the unfortunate demolition of James Donald's gushet at the **Auld Toll House** (1895-96). But there is much that is tawdry and mean, too, especially in Lawn Street and Silk

Street where only **no. 2** (c. 1810) has been saved by a bold, if heavy-handed, rehabilitation.

Beyond Thomas Baird's neo-Romanesque **St Mirin's Cathedral** (1930-32) a second phase of New Town building occurred along the road to Glasgow. **1, 8, 10** and **12 Glasgow Road** and **9-11 Christie Street** (all early 19th century) are ashlar tenements with street door flats and round stair towers at the
63 rear. **3-19 Glasgow Road** (c. 1820), however, assume a more urbane elegance in a long symmetrical terrace of two-storey-and-basement houses with Corinthian columned porches at **3, 11** and **19**. But nothing else was built — apart, that is, from the linear weaving village of Williamsburgh further east — until new ranges of Thomsonesque tenements began to spread along Glasgow Road, first at **Royal Terrace** and **Greenlaw Terrace** (c. 1885) and later in **Greenlaw Avenue**.

64 **Greenlaw House**
(1774)

Robert Corse's country residence was built *three stories high; which he has finished in the completest manner of good ashlar-work, and the stones well polished, adorned with an ionic cornice, and a concave door, built after the Corinthian order, fronting the west, balustraded on the top, crowned with vases ... the two square wings are leaded on the top, ballustraded and crowned with vases also, beautified with two Venetian windows in front ...* Semple's 1782 description serves still, though the house has acquired a porch and a streetful of Late Victorian neighbours. Not far to the north at **38 Mansionhouse Road** is a late 18th century *Gothick* building with a birdcage bellcote, probably an outbuilding of Corse's mansion.

Two red sandstone churches stand on this northern
65 side of Glasgow Road. **Greenlaw Church** (1888-89), by Abercrombie and Symington, is an aisleless nave with three lancets and a single apex quatrefoil in its west gable. James Donald's **Sherwood Church** (1891-92; hall by Hamilton Neil 1925; spire 1927) is less distinguished by its Perpendicular Gothic than by the slender perpendicular of its cruelly shorn spire. Next door is McCambridge and Torrance's Postmodernist showroom for **Hampden Cars** (1984), a glazed cylinder set slickly against polychromatic brick.

66 **McKerrell Street** (c. 1890-1900) has a splendid range of tenements repeating the details of Royal Terrace from **2-14** but undulating in carved corbelled bays from **24-50**. **Crossflat Crescent** is similar but bowed from the ground up with unusual *bracket profile* lintels. Here, too, there is a church; though bricked up as an industrial store, W. D. McLennan's
67 **Ralston U.P. Church** (1899-1904) barely merits the

Top 3-19 Glasgow Road.
Middle Greenlaw House with outbuilding below.
Above McKerrell Street tenements.

Renfrew District

Paisley Museum

Paisley Museum

Strathclyde Region

Carson & Hunter

68

RCAHMS

69

Top Anchor Recreation Club Pavilion.
Above Kilnside House c. 1900.

name. Cottage-like beside the tenements, its slated roofs spill down over low entrances on Cyril Street and Violet Street.

Anchor Mills

Unlike Coats' Ferguslie Mills, manufacturing is still underway here at Clark's Mills in Seedhill. Like Ferguslie, most of the working buildings are by the Bradford firm, Woodhouse and Morley. The **Finishing Mill** (1886) and the **Mile End Mill** (1899-1900) are both five-storey brick boxes with the customary top storey of round-arched windows, eaves cornice, and arcuated or fretted balustrading. Abercrombie and Maitland's **Anchor Recreation Club** (1924-25) is appropriately neither urban nor industrial: the back-to-back pavilions are identical, each like some elevated Elizabethan Inn raised above the playing fields. Also in the Anchor grounds in **Kilnside House** (c. 1830), now the Cue Ball Club, a late Georgian house with a wide pedimented porch of four Ionic columns and a balustraded area.

Glasgow Road continues eastwards through Williamsburgh. Nothing of the pre-Victorian village remains; instead, a few last ranges of tenements. The **Burgh Bar** (1905), by Brand and Lithgow, at Lacy Street has a fairy-tale gingerbread-house look, while **Harvie's Bar**, at 86 Glasgow Road, has some fine sign-writing. The **Kelburne Cinema** (1923-33), last of Paisley's picture houses, is a blocky Mayan mass by W. Taylor.

By the time Barshaw Park is reached, suburbia has begun. Through Oldhall and Ralston bourgeois sprawl stretches to the Glasgow boundary and beyond; but there are some surprises all but swamped by the morass of bungalows and semi-dets. **St Mark's Church** is red-brick Italian Romanesque, complete with wheel window and heavy hooded porch. **Penilee**

70

Anchor Mills seen across the river White Cart.

Carson & Hunter

Sports Pavilion is suitably streamlined and airy, full of Thirties' *logic and light*. **Ralston Golf Clubhouse** (c. 1800), on the other hand, musters as much Neoclassical elegance as the converted stableblock of David Hamilton's **Ralston House** (1810, demolished 1934) will allow. The later estate lodge houses by Campbell Douglas and Stevenson also remain as private residences: **West Lodge** (1865), 226 Glasgow Road, and **East Lodge** (1865) at Crookston Drive.

Infectious Diseases Hospital, Hawkhead, in the 1930s.

Hawkhead Hospital
Thomas S. Tait (1932-35)
Some way south of Ralston golf course and across the White Cart lie the much altered pavilions of the former infectious diseases hospital on Hawkhead Road. How ironical that the anatomy of this building should have been so diseased by neglect and abuse — and poignantly so, since its architect, one of the pioneers of British Modernism, was himself Paisley-born and bred.

Thomas S. Tait *(1882-1954) was educated in Paisley at the John Neilson Institution. First apprenticed with James Donald, he studied at the School of Art in Glasgow before joining the prestigious office of J. J. Burnet in 1904. By 1918 he was a partner, establishing Burnet, Tait and Lorne in the vanguard of British Modernism. In the 1930s he made his mark in Scotland at the 1938 Empire Exhibition in Glasgow; in Edinburgh, where he designed St Andrew's House, "Scotland's most prominent 1930s building"; in the streamlined wards of Hawkhead I.D. Hospital (q.v.) in his home-town; and at Johnstone (q.v.) where, according to the then Secretary of State, he made a "magnificent effort . . . to secure greatly improved amenities with first class architecture in our housing schemes".*

Penilee Sports Pavilion.

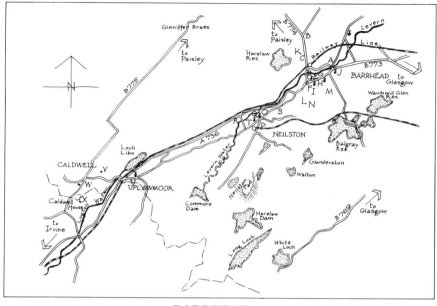

BARRHEAD

It is difficult to find any heart to Barrhead. In part this is simply a consequence of the town's origin as "congeries of villages" — strung together by the precipitate surge of industry along the Levern Valley some two centuries ago. But it is also the result of industry's canker: abandoned factories, half-demolished bridges and viaducts, windswept gap sites, boarded-up shops and houses.

The Levern, of course, still flows through the centre of town. No longer the *busiest river in Scotland* it was two hundred years ago, it is at least less fetid than McDonald found it on one of his *Rambles Round Glasgow* in the middle of last century.

> *A sadly tortured stream . . . what with dams and lades; mill wheels and colouring matters of every hue with which it is fretted and stained, it has a really pitiable common-sewer aspect. . . .*

"Barrhead, you must understand, has undergone a considerable metamorphosis with these thirty years back . . . then it consisted of thirty families, now there is a street half a mile in length, built on each side . . . there was perhaps but one small cotton factory on the Levern, and now there are six large ones . . . thirty years ago there was only one public house in this village and now there are certainly thirty. . . ."
(From Taylor, C., The Levern Delineated, Glasgow, 1831, p. 72.)

Almost all the mills, bleachfields and printing works that once clogged its course have gone, as have many later foundries and factories. On the road to Neilston **Gateside Mill** (1786) still functions, though no longer to spin cotton, while on the other side of town, a few low rubble walls are all that remain of the Laigh or **Levern Mill** (1780), first cotton spinning mill on the river and second in the whole of Scotland. But between the two, through the centre of Barrhead, the Levern winds across a scarred landscape which, though it has begun to heal, invites no one.

Enclosing this inert open heart, a triangle of streets — Carlibar Road, Cross Arthurlie Street and Main Street — sustains some sense of urban life, though with little consistency of scale and even less spatial enclosure.

Carlibar Road is open, even suburban, particularly close to Levern Mill, where the grounds of **Carlibar House** (demolished 1976) form a pleasant wooded enclave between road and river. More urban are a few remaining tenements : **34-38** have consoled close entries and first floor windows cornices, but it is their three-storey scale, matching the raised railway opposite, which matters most.

Beyond the railway, vestiges of the town's village origins crop up, even if, like the crisp farm form of
B **Crosstobs Inn** or the equally plain **Craigiebar** (c. 1820), 75 Paisley Road, they are all but buried by the march of bungalow and semi-detached. At **Dealston House,** 64 Paisley Road, something of a Scotstyle pastiche, the scale rises to three-storeys while, closer to the tracks, at **1-19 Paisley Road** and
C **4-8 Graham Street,** a vast corner block of bayed tenements in red and ochre sandstone, built in 1901 for the Co-op., it reaches a robust four.

Top Craigiebar, 75 Paisley Road.
Above Co-operative Society tenements, Paisley Road/Graham Street.

Cross Arthurlie Street is thoroughly urban — though breached by decay and demolition. Tucked in against the railway viaduct is **The Brig Inn** with chamferred and roll-moulded rybats to the windows at first floor and a corbelled third storey of round-arched bargeboarded dormers. But tenements predominate. At **100-104 Cross Arthurlie Street** (c. 1875) the top storey has been modelled with the incipient pilaster details of a Thomsonesque eaves, while **62** and **74** still carry fascias in signwriter's copperplate. Further on, at **35-47** (c. 1830) a dilapidated stretch of the town's earliest streetscape survives: two-storey gable-to-gable shops and housing with the occasional front wall chimney. Cochrane Street dips and rises past
D McWhannell and Rogerson's **Masonic Temple** (1910) to connect with **Main Street,** the third side of the triangle defining the centre of town.

Main Street is at first stolidly Victorian. Ashlar tenements, two-storey houses with attic bays, and finally, raised above the present street level, the disused halls and kirk of **Westbourne Church** (c. 1850?), a severe seven-windowed box returning to a three bay front with parapetted cornice and a solid ashlar porch. Across the street a few rundown houses maintain street enclosure.

Masonic Temple, Cochrane Street.

Bourock Church.

With a few months *of the opening of the Bourock Church its congregation had rejected dependence on Neilston Parish Church (q.v.), the local farmers had retaliated by rioting on Main Street and the minister had led his people to a sand pit behind the church building where they continued to meet as Dissenters. It was after all the year of the Disruption! Not until 1850 did the Bourock Church open again.*

Sports Centre.

E **Bourock Parish Church**
James Stuart (?) (1843)
The church has a T-plan with staircase vestibules set in the internal angles and, over the main entrance, a tall belfried steeple with octagonal spire. Despite the vertical feel, intensified by the fall of the land to the north and the slenderness of the steeple to the south, the stylistic idiom is not pointed Gothic but elongated Norman. The single-storey hall extension to the east (1930), linked to the old *Madras* school in the church basement is by William Baillie.

F   **Arthurlie Parish Church** (1967), a clerestorey-lit orange brick box by Honeyman, Jack and Robertson tries hard to realise the potential of its raised corner site. From the church the prospect along Main Street exposes all the misfortunes of open-heart surgery which Barrhead has had to suffer. To the left, the original street has disappeared and the view bleeds out into the specious success of urban reclamation. Set back in carpark tarmac a new **Health Centre** (1980-81) by the Cunningham Glass Partnership and a

G   bulky **Sports Centre** (1977-78) by James Cunningham have been built, but neither provides the mix of function that might animate the street nor, indeed, the kind of small-scale aggregative composition needed to respond to the buildings opposite. This southern side of the street is at least partially intact; two-storey slated 19th century houses and shops — the nearest thing left to the old Barrhead *raws*. **80-108 Main Street** (c. 1840) preserve some early shopfronts; **114-120** are later with architraves to the windows and an odd octagonal chimney stack at **118; 130-136** (c. 1875) are somewhat grander with recessed stub pilasters and capitals *à la* Thomson to each first-floor window; oldest of all, **138-140** (c. 1780-1800) have a pediment rising from the eaves line. On the corner of Bank Street is a **Bank of Scotland** (1979), black, brash and for no good reason hexagonal in plan form.

Renfrew District

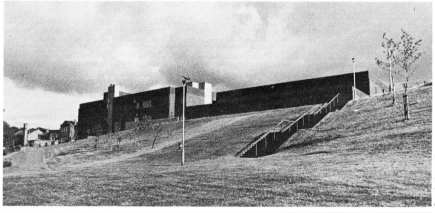

Cunningham, Glass

Carson & Hunter

Police Buildings, Main Street.

H **Police Buildings**
McWhannell and Rogerson (1902-04)
At 124-128 Main Street — sheer bravura! Designed as
ebullient neighbours, these red sandstone excursions
into an absurdly extravagant Baronial Revival are still
*the only public buildings in Barrhead of any architectural
merit*: crowsteps, strapwork, corbelling, dormers,
heraldic panel, high tower — everything is there, plus
a hint of *Art Nouveau* in the hinges of the studded
yett entrance at no. 124.

South Church (1846), formerly the Free Church,
its astylar facade so naïvely composed as to defy
description, invites perverse affection. This block of
building from Ralston Road to Arthurlie Street is the
best of old Barrhead. There is a classically simple
I single-storey house at **17 Cloth Street** and, behind
J the trees and gardens of **Lowndes Street,** several
cottage villas and mansions much varied in style
surprise the passer-by with their tarnished elegance.
From Arthurlie Street east, however, everything is
new, architecturally poor, but sensible enough to
perpetuate the alignment of the street's earlier older
buildings. Finally, where Carlibar Road closes the
triangle around the Levern, comes **St John's Church**
(1960) by Alex. McInally, a tall brick building, on a
cruciform plan, with a detached brick belfry tower —
vaguely Scandinavian.

Levern and Nitshill Church
(1835)
North of **Waterside Bridge** (c. 1780), a twin-arched
span bridged by the railway viaduct, the church is
isolated in the open country of Levernside, a plain

Levern and Nitshill Church.

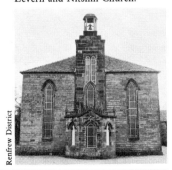

Renfrew District

hip-roofed building, three hooded lancets long, with a thin front "tower" rising from a battlemented porch to support an open ogee-capped hexagonal belfry. At the rear is a low vestry and to the south a detached hall (1895) cleverly incorporating a narrow gable window similar to that in the church's tower.

Churches are not the only buildings of distinction to be found. Some of the houses of the wealthy — landowner or millowner — survive, though not all as the *handsome mansions, generally surrounded by umbrageous timber* they once were.

Chappell House stables.

Chappell House (c. 1757) built by Mr Graham, owner of the first bleachfield in the valley, stands above the left bank of the Levern, on the hillier west side of town. Still residential, it is a two-storey gabled house, roughcast with dressed surrounds, architecturally diminished by subsequent recasting and extension. In the grounds **St Conval's Well** can be found and there is a symmetrical stables block (c. 1770) leading into the yard of which is a central arched pend surmounted by a pediment on top of which stands the sculptured form of a greyhound.

Trees (c. 1760), now the clubhouse of Fereneze Golf Course, also sits on rising ground above the river. Taylor, writing in 1831, found it *richly ornamented* but it has lost the decorative timber verandah he depicted and is now a rather austere pavilion-roofed block with a dentilled eaves and Roman Doric doorpiece.

Arthurlie House (c. 1780), on the Levern's right bank, is surrounded on all sides by new housing. Now a community centre, it retains its wooded setting. The model is two-storey-and-basement Georgian, lacking a pediment, but with blind arch recesses framing the windows and a broad bridging stair rising to a twin-columned porch. To the right of the house is a single-storey wing possibly added when Henry Dunlop, owner of the Levern Mill (*q.v.*), acquired the house in 1818.

The name *Arthurlie* is a recurring puzzle in Barrhead not only in its derivation but in its application too.

Nether Arthurlie.

It appears there was originally but one place of this name and in the course of time this has branched off to East, West, South, mid, Nether . . . and so on, which puzzles many . . .

The dilemma in nomenclature remains, for **Nether Arthurlie** (c. 1810), now part of St Mary's Convent, has been variously labelled, East Arthurlie, Arthurlie Proper, and Arthurlie House. A small chapel (1925) and a considerable amount of indifferent residential

Arthurlie House.

accommodation (1927, 1965-68) have been built in the grounds but the original house is almost intact and certainly impressive. It is a three-storey pavilion-roofed mansion with a columned porch and symmetrical single-storey wings. A fluted frieze unites porch and wings and also appears over the windows of the first floor.

South Arthurlie (from 1735), on Grampian Way, is a wholly irregular aggregation of simpler vernacular forms! To the right is a low crow-step gabled house with a 1735 marriage stone over what was the original central entrance but has since become a wider window; in the middle, a higher Victorian block to which has been added a slated ogee-roofed porch; and to the left, a gabled billiard room wing. This long front is unified by a consistent use of stone and slate and relates well with similar buildings which frame the garden on the west.

Levernholme, off the Glasgow Road some distance north of Barrhead, is now an old folks' home known as Tinto House. Approached over an arched bridge with unusual *waffle* parapets (c. 1780), the house is notable not so much for its Georgian form and detail — though there is a superb porch — as for the remarkable wing which the Coats family added in 1902. Carried out in grandiloquent style the Baroque quality of the exterior is matched by the lavish interior of the billiard room which takes up the whole of the first floor: richly carved wood, marble ingle-neuk fireplace, a barrel vaulted ceiling of floral plasterwork and a series of stained glass panels on the theme of King Lear. For this — and much more in Barrhead — Lear's own words seem to ring ironically true:

The art of our necessities is strange
That can make vile things precious.

NEILSTON

Neilston Parish Church.

Paisley Central Library

NEILSTON
0 **Neilston Parish Church**
(from 1762)

The church is one of seven ancient foundations in
Renfrewshire (the others were Inchinnan Templars,
Killallan, Renfrew, Pollokshaws, St Mirin's at Paisley
and St Winoc's at Lochwinnoch) all of which antedate
the emergence of Paisley Abbey as the dominant
religious house in the county. The present kirk, begun
in 1762-63 and later widened and heightened by a
local wright, William Lamb, in 1796-98, is
characteristically 18th century in form — a pavilion-
roofed 5-bay-square building with an inset ogee-capped
belfry rising in three stages out of a hip-roofed porch
which has been added around its base. Placed above
the burial vault of the Mures of Caldwell, a single
traceried window, possibly 17th century, has been
incorporated from an earlier church. Otherwise,
window forms and moulding details are classically
severe; meet metaphor perhaps for the strait-laced,
straight-backed rigours of Presbyterian worship. Stiff-
necked, too, the Neilston parishioners: unwilling to
thole the heritors' demands for seat rents, the
congregation once gathered for eight years in the
churchyard where the minister preached from a
wooden pulpit. Not until 1831, when the House of
Lords had had to make a final pronouncement in their
favour, did the parishioners return.

46

Though the glebe has greatly diminished —
including the loss of the **Manse** (c. 1776) in 1976 —
the graveyard surrounding the church is still extensive
and contains several early tombstones bearing so-called
runic knots. Unique in Renfrewshire is the conjunction
of two circular gatehouses to the kirk yard: that to the
left is the older (pre-1789), while the larger, to the
right, probably dates from the early 19th century.
Both have conical slated roofs with circular chimney
stacks. No doubt at different times they would
function as mort-house, watch house, offertory or
session house.

St Thomas's Church (1861, tower 1891), 70
Main Street, has little to recommend it architecturally
and is in any case compromised by an ugly porch and
the clumsy bulk of its adjacent school (1904). On
High Street is the former **Free Church** (1873) by
Campbell Douglas and Sellars, since 1964 serving as
the Parish Church Hall; five round-arched windows
long, minimally early Norman in style.

Worthier of notice is the red sandstone facade of
the **Glen Halls** (1898) at 8-10 Main Street, a
composition of Tudor window groupings balanced
almost symmetrically about a gabled frontispiece: *very
handsome* was the verdict of Neilston's principal
historian Dr Pride when he wrote about the village in
1910. Dr Pride's own house, once a bank and now the
Masonic Lodge, sits across the street. Stricter in
symmetry and classical detail, it still has an arrogantly
alien grandeur of scale. More recent community
buildings, floating in off-street isolation nearby, seem
rather mean and bleak by comparison. The white-
walled **Library** (1980), by T. M. Miller and Partners,
has a neat Modernist monopitch with a recessed
parapet fascia in copper, but it is difficult to escape
the feeling that what has been achieved in this new
leisure enclave is a kind of shame-faced architectural
limbo-land shuffling away from the real street life of
the village.

Top Glen Halls.
Above Masonic Lodge.

What has been going on at the centre of Neilston
is a prolonged outbreak of indecent exposure. In every
respect, McDonald's 1856 assessment that here was *a
compact, neat and withal somewhat old-fashioned little
township* has been completely reversed. Along Main
Street to Holehouse Brae demolition and road re-
alignment have removed the built-up enclosures of the
past. Two indifferent tenement blocks have been
saved: **55-63 Main Street** (c. 1870) two-storeyed with
a replacement storey of hipped dormers; and at
101-109 (c. 1890) an even plainer three-storeyed run
of shops and twin-windowed flats. A row of terrace
houses at **12-18** (c. 1840?), with pilastered doorpieces
at **14** and **18,** and several swept dormers, runs hard to
the heel of the pavement; as does the **Victoria Bar**

Houses in Main Street.

(c. 1825) round the corner in Bank Street, a two-storeyed house with central pediment and stack. Some ill-conceived shopping infill cancels out these vestiges of the old streetscape and, though the Victorian **Clydesdale Bank** can at least afford the street some Corinthian pilasters, it is not until three single-storey slated cottages, gable-to-gable at **86-90**, that the feel of the *little township* returns. The mix of dwellings continues, but **142-146,** despite earnestly insensitive rehabilitation, manage to reiterate the right scale. Finally, on both sides of Uplawmoor Road come several streets of single- and two-storey brick terraces, minimal accommodation built for the millworkers at Crofthead. Not everyone here now works in the mills; but some do, for downhill at **Crofthead Works** cotton thread and synthetic fibre production still maintains the industrial tradition of Leverndale. Although the original mill of 1792 burnt down in 1883, the vast storeyed brick bulk of Mills No. 2 (1880) and No. 3 (1881) — the former with an unusual elliptically planned staircase tower — continue to dominate the rural scene in the valley below. As for the millworkers' rows, they have become an exciting riot of contingent colour and material with every kind of window, door and dormer alteration, the whole somehow still bound together by the close-packed stepping terrace forms and the single consistent decorative feature — a corbel-blocked eaves.

Behind the village's long main street there is

Nether Kirkton House.

nothing but a dismal accumulation of characterless housing. Only a few buildings rise above this generally dreary background. Hidden in trees off Neilston Road is **Nether Kirkton House** (1898) a rather erect two-storey and basement Renaissance mansion. At the other end of the village is the earlier **High Crofthead House,** tall too, and brutally plain and white, looking for all the world like something a child might have drawn. But the most charming dwelling in Neilston is **Broadlie House** (c. 1830?), a long cottage villa with attic dormers and a surprisingly narrow columned porch, the pedimented entablature of which continues along the full length of the facade. Against each gable are lower hipped wings only one of which now extends round the yard at the rear.

Below Broadlie House.
Bottom Millworkers' rows.

UPLAWMOOR

Uplawmoor is not much more than a one-street village stretching along the high road from Neilston to Lugton. For the most part it is genteel — now more suburban than rural. Nevertheless, despite inter-war sprawl, clues to the village's origins are still to be found in the cluster of single-storey houses grouped around the junction of Neilston Road with Tannoch Road. While one or two of these cottages may once have housed the miners who, until the earlier years of last century, worked the coal shafts cut into the wooded hillside above Loch Libo, it seems more likely that most were built for the estate workers of the local laird, Mure of Caldwell. Perhaps two hundred years old (though one property at least can trace its title back more than three centuries) these simple rubble-built dwellings give the west end of the main street some semblance of rural character.

At Neukfoot, where until not so long ago a cruck-roofed cottage still stood, **8-10 Neilston Road** preserve something of the first streetscape. The **Post Office**, too, is long with skewed gables and chimney stacks moulded to cover the thatch that must have covered the roofs of most of these plain buildings. Slates are no disfigurement but the same cannot be said for the widened windows. **Uplaw Cottage** across the street has had attic bays added; **Thorn Cottage** has a long but not too intrusive dormer; **Finniebrae** has lost its central doorway; while **West Crossgates** has been romanticised by the addition of patterned shutters, tile sills, bull-nose panes and leaded glass. Further along the street, **Uplawmoor Hotel** (c. 1750?) formerly The Inn, comprises the old coaching inn, a two-storey three-bay house and a longer extension (c. 1958) which, while it maintains the inn's roof slope and the wallplane of the upper storey, pushes forward inelegantly at ground floor. Above this projection the open terrace is protected by *Art Nouveau* railings skilfully derived by architect James Gray from Mackintosh, long before the present cult of popular adulation. **Bridgend House**, at the north-east limit of the village, low but two-storeyed, once housed five families, the two upper flats of the tenement reached by two external stairs at the rear. Next door, **Bridgend** is also two-storey but higher; now roughcast and shuttered, it was originally another single-storey cottage.

Caldwell Parish Church (1888) by William Ingram is a low buttressed hall in grey sandstone presenting its bellcoted and lancetted entrance gable to the street. The **Community Centre** (1876), formerly the local school, has decorative bargeboards over its boys' and girls' entrance porches and to its hipped end

Below West Crossgates.
Bottom Caldwell Parish Church.

Carson & Hunter

Paisley Central Library

gable. A timber *flèche* over the central ridge ventilator has been removed but attractively fretted ridge tiles survive. Across Mure Place is the former **School House** (1877), 49 Neilston Road, similarly detailed, with a central stub-columned gabled porch.

Tower of Caldwell juts out of the hillside by Old Barn Farm, west of the village, across the valley of the Lugton Water. Square in plan, it rises through three storeys, the two lower of which are stone vaulted, to a battlemented parapet. Access can be gained directly to the ground floor chamber while an L-plan forestair reaches first floor before climbing in the thickness of the wall to the uppermost storey. Most of the masonry is in good condition thanks to repeated restorations and repairs but the origin of the tower remains problematical. Dates of 15th century and 16th century have been suggested and it may be that the foundations derive from the mediaeval castle of the Mures of Caldwell. Of this ancient building, however, nothing — or nothing else — remains. For after William Mure's disastrous involvement with the Covenanters in 1666 and his subsequent flight abroad, the estate was forfeited and given to General Tam Dalziel of The Binns *in whose possession the house of Caldwell fell into disrepair.* A generation later in 1698 the Mures recovered their lands but a decade after this the castle was reported still in ruins. Robertson, writing in 1818, refers fleetingly to *the old Castle of Caldwell, of which only the principal tower is now standing.* Whether, and indeed why, this solitary keep was rebuilt during the 18th century is difficult to determine. What can be said is that instead of restoring their old home the Mures moved half a mile or so west to **Hall of Caldwell** — an 18th century gabled house (later much extended) standing behind a high garden wall into which an arched portal from the former buildings had been inserted — and to **Caldwell House** (1773), a late example of the early castle manner of Robert and James Adam, which William Baron Mure had built as the new family seat just across the county boundary in Ayrshire.

Carson & Hunter

Top Tower of Caldwell.
Above Hall of Caldwell.

Caldwell House.

RCAHMS

Wallace Buildings before their demolition in 1973-74.

The Wallace Memorial.

Renfrew District

ELDERSLIE

Elderslie boasts an ancient and, by association, heroic history. The Scottish patriot Sir William Wallace (c. 1270-1305) was born here — though not in the so-called **Wallace Buildings** which stood until 1973-74 at 243 Main Road. Despite the persistent claims of local legend, these were merely the rump of the 17th century Wallace Farm. The retention of their foundations on a grassy mound is rather casual and tawdry. The **Wallace Memorial** (1912), John G. T. Murray and J. Andrew Minty, is certainly grand in grey granite but, conventionally based on a medieval mercat cross theme, just as surely dull.

Despite some coal mining carried on until the middle of last century, and cotton spinning on the Brandy Burn, latterly supplanted by paper and carpet manufacture, Elderslie has sunk into suburban anonymity. Main Road runs the length of the village in a succession of tenements, villas, cottages and bungalows. Near the junction with Glenpatrick Road, however, some early 19th century character can still be sensed in a few older buildings.

Wallace Tavern, 183 Main Road, is the best of these — a two-storey house-pub with shouldered chimney stack on the front and turnpike stair behind. The **Moat House**, in crow-stepped vernacular, flatters to deceive: the stone is too crisply cut, the window lintels too wide. Built 1903, it incorporates older elements in its interior and a 1727 marriage stone in the garden. Nearby is **Glen Gardens** (1983-84), an attractive cluster of monopitched orange brick sheltered housing by John Laird. The **Wallace School** (c. 1866-1890) still stands on Main Road, a gaunt testimony to the bleak ordeals of primary education last century, while an earlier school building (1799) has become the local **Library** in Stoddard Square. The **Village Hall** (1881), single-storey-and-attic with crow-stepped doorpiece and central gable, was funded by the American-born Arthur Francis Stoddard (1810-82) whose initiative converted Glenpatrick Mill into a prosperous carpet factory.

Elderslie Parish Church (1840, 1885-86), 284 Main Road, is a sturdy grey stone kirk with belfried gable front. **Elderslie East Church** (1898-1900), formerly the Free Church, on Glenpatrick Road, is in a more Decorated red sandstone Gothic. This is the first ecclesiastical work by William D. McLennan and, while it does not compare with his later St Matthew's, Paisley (*q.v.*), the light open trusses over the nave and detailing of some of the interior woodwork betray his growing interest in Glasgow Style idiom.

Below Glen Gardens housing. **Bottom** Elderslie East Church drawn by T. A. Moodie.

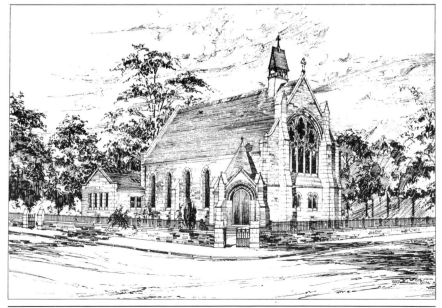

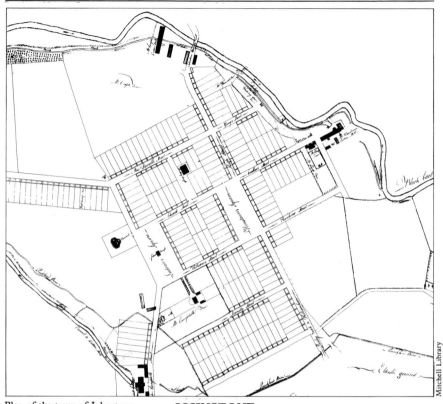

Mitchell Library

Plan of the town of Johnstone
drawn by N. Snodgrass, 1796.

JOHNSTONE

The most perceptible physical aspect of Johnstone is
its regularised street layout. The original feuing plan
(1782), by Paisley architect, surveyor and antiquarian
Charles Ross, aligned the street pattern on the old
route from Thorn Brae down to the bridge over the
Black Cart Water, locating the town on *good dry land*
between the riverside mills and the coal pits of
Quarrelton to the south. Two open squares —
Houston Square and Ludovic Square — were
incorporated and the emergent grid-iron reinforced by
east-west streets along the north and south sides of the
new town.

Johnstone Mill; Old End to the
right.

Renfrew District

 Johnstone Mill (1782) still stands at the six-storey
Old End of Paton's Mill, Mill Brae, while at **Cartside
Mill** (1790), a mile or so to the west where the road
to Kilbarchan crosses the river, there is another six-
storey cast-iron structure rather more architecturally
developed with two semi-octagonal bays to the south
and Palladian windows similarly positioned on the
opposite north front.

 Industrial expansion — first textiles, later machine
tools — produced a rapid increase in population, *not
exceeded if equalled in the annals of Scottish history*

according to the Second Statistical Account of 1835.
The *neat and regularly built village* of the 1790s
succumbed to a mix of backlands development.
Cobbett, lecturing here in 1832, still found a *very nice
little manufacturing town* — but by mid-century
foundry, mill, cottage and tenement were packed
together cheek by jowl. A visitor in 1853 remarked
that

> *Johnstone has by no means a lively or inviting
> appearance. It is neither picturesque nor elegant. It
> has a forbidding look, dinginess pervades the plain
> and cheap-looking architecture.*

A generation later Groome's *Gazetteer* is less damning,
though hardly complimentary:

> *The houses are substantial stone buildings and viewed
> from a distance the place has a remarkably airy
> appearance, due in part to the spaciousness of the
> streets and in part to the number of pieces of open
> garden-ground attached to the houses; but on closer
> inspection a good deal of the dinginess always
> associated with manufactures becomes at once
> apparent.*

Continuous runs of two-storey gable-to-gable
housing, generally with central shouldered chimney
stacks, can be found at **11-19 High Street**, where two
houses are pedimented; at **22-32**; at **63-67**; and at
10-12 Collier Street where shop fronts and fascia are
almost intact. There are a few similar individual
houses left: the bow-fronted **Thorn Inn** (c. 1810)
marks the eastern entrance to the town on the gushet
site between Thorn Brae and Beith Road; **35 William
Street** and the red-rendered **31 Brewery Street** are

31 and 35 William Street.

Renfrew District

Strathclyde Region

Renfrew District

more or less detached; **66** and **70 High Street** are sandwiched between higher development, the latter carrying the date 1810 in a rope mould ellipse in its pediment. **62**, **64** and **68 High Street** are in the same vein but three-storeyed; **62** is the finest with moulded architraves and a curved gablet supporting the customary central stack, The **Black Bull Inn** at 72 High Street, particularly valuable since it may have antedated the town plan of 1782, was demolished in 1985.

Mixed in with this streetfront building are a few set-back early houses: some a full two storeys, like **19 Laighcartside Street** with consoled doorway and soffit blocks below the eaves; others such as **31 William Street** or **8 Laighcartside Street**, which has pilastered attic dormers, are lower cottage villas. Tenements intrude too: **80 High Street** in later red sandstone, catches the eye through *Art Nouveau* motifs cut in the stone at street level and in the fascia timber of The Millbrae Inn. Roughly contemporary, on Thorn Brae at the other end of the town, **1-3 Lindsay Place** (c. 1900) is more idiosyncratic — perhaps the work of William D. McLennan.

Houston Square ought to be — but isn't — elegant. There is a preponderance of *Woolworth Moderne*. Robust mouldings and gabled dormers at **42 High Street** (1877) do, however, provide some Victorian vigour on the north side, and the **Bandstand** (1891), by James B. Lamb — a gift *from the laird* as its paternalistic inscription tersely records — is at least light and frothy on its open ironwork.

Ludovic Square, intended as a market place, has fine villas and, stopping the axis of Church Street and dominating the town's skyline with its eponymously high spire, a fine parish church.

Houston Square

RCAHMS

Opposite top High Street with the Black Bull Inn (demolished 1983) to the left.
Middle 1-3 Lindsay Place, Thorn Brae.
Bottom Houston Square.

High Parish Church.

High Parish Church
(1792-94)

This elongated octagonal church building lit by two pointed windows on each of its rubble-walled faces, has an ashlar tower in front, also octagonal, rising above the entrance in two castellated stages to its 1823 needle spire. Focused on table and pulpit, it is a thoroughly Scots kirk, right down to the two sermon-checking clocks still ticking on opposite faces of the wrap-round gallery (internal remodelling and vestry by David Thomson, 1875).

The **East Parish Church** (1828-29), Walkinshaw Street, was first of all the Relief Church, a five-light hall kirk in rubble with a later three-door Renaissance porch (c. 1910) in rusticated ashlar (note the *Art Nouveau* leaded glasswork). **St Paul's**, Church Street (1906) has a traceried gable front in early perpendicular. **St Margaret's** (1852), Graham Street, has some charm, largely the result of the finely cut stone work of W. R. and S. Ingram's 1875 double transept additions.

The **District Council Offices** (1887), by Charles Davidson, formerly municipal offices and police court, insert some Scots Baronial into Collier Street. Next door the domed front of the **Masonic Lodge** (1912) affects an absurdly scaled-down pretension, halfway between 19th century vulgarity and 20th century

St Paul's Church.

Carson & Hunter

Carson & Hunter

Renfrew District

Top Globe Cinema.
Above The Bird in the Hand.

Johnstone Castle as it was
illustrated in A. H. Millar's *Castles
& Mansions of Renfrewshire*, 1889.

austerity. All the way to Thirties' Modernism is the
old **Globe Cinema** (c. 1939) at the corner of High
Street and Canal Street — four full-height fins project
from the streamlined curve above the entrance; the tall
windows are patterned in series of arrow-head
astragals; there is a marvellous *Yachting Style* shop. It
needs more than bingo to sustain it.

Thomas S. Tait's **Howwood Road Housing**
(from 1935) beyond Quarrelton had parapetted roofs
and horizontal glazing bars before they disappeared in
dubious rehabilitation. Close by, **The Bird in the
Hand** (c. 1910), by T. G. Abercrombie, retains some
of the sociable English virtues of a turn-of-the-century
Arts and Crafts inn.

Johnstone Castle

Across the Beith Road are the lands of Easter
Cochrane, home of the Houstouns from 1733 when
the family moved from their estate at Milliken,
retaining its original name of Johnstone for this new
demesne. The old house was altered in 1771 and again
in 1812, by George Houstoun, the enterprising fourth
laird who transformed Johnstone Place into the
battlemented **Johnstone Castle**. The work may have
been carried out by James Gillespie Graham whose
castellated country houses were, like Johnstone, *given
a picturesque outline by the addition of a large round
tower at one end*. The building was demolished in 1950
but its central square tower was preserved along with
a crow-stepped bartizaned portion of earlier work
bearing a sundial dated 1700. This odd conjunction
stands on a grassy knoll in Tower Place, hidden away
at the middle of a maze of 1950s local authority
housing.

RCAHMS

RIAS

Cochrane Castle, less than a mile to the west, was already in ruins when the Houstouns were building Johnstone. In 1896, however, George Ludovic Houstoun had a small crow-stepped tower erected to mark the site. The tower, which incorporates a stone relic with the Cochrane arms and the date 1592, stands at Auchengreoch Road in the grounds of the **Red House** (1896-97), an Arts and Crafts essay in hard red brick and black and white half-timbering, by Charles Davidson.

Howwood Road housing as originally proposed.

In September 1848, the Polish composer Frederick Chopin, escaping revolutionary events in Paris, arrived at Johnstone Castle as the guest of Ludovic Houston, the Fifth Laird, whose daughter was studying music. But, exhausted by his travels in Britain and the enthusiastic demands laid on him by his hosts, he grew ill; "hysterically, at last, he hurried back to Paris".

Renfrew District

Johnstone Castle; ruined vestiges in Tower Place.

RCAHMS

Top High Barholm.
Above Cartside Terrace.

Carson & Hunter

View from Low Barholm.

Renfrew District

KILBARCHAN
Milliken Park

A At Waterside, where the road from Johnstone crosses the Black Cart Water, the architectural character of Kilbarchan village is already clear. **3 Cartside Terrace** (1796) is a plain rubble-built house with dressed margins, though a third storey in a central chimneyed gable front raises it above the prevailing eaves height of most of Kilbarchan's houses.

B On Milliken Park Road along the river bank there is an interlude of Victorian villas. **Tower House** (c. 1850) is heavily quoined with narrow round-arched windows, a dumpy square tower and later single-storey wing by Alexander Kirkland. **Ashburn** (c. 1850), formerly Ashbank, is taller with high dormers and a particularly attractive, if incongruous, stable block in textured polychromatic brick. **Glencart House** (c. 1840), also by Kirkland, has a splendid cast iron verandah along its riverside front.

C **Beaufort** (1909), by Kerr and Watson, and the three gabled front of **Hillhouse** (1906), by James Kennedy Shanks, both on Tandlehill Road, are typical turn-of-the-century Anglicised suburban.

Low and High Barholm

The older village is not reached until **Low Barholm** and **High Barholm** where the true Kilbarchan townscape emerges: on both sides of the street, two-storey houses — each once both home and weaving shop — pack side by side, unified in scale, material and detail, but never entirely identical. Several

properties carry dates cut in the pediments or shouldered bases of street front chimney stacks — 1825, 1827, 1836, etc. **34 High Barholm** (1826) has an excellent pilastered doorpiece. Generally the low two-storey scale predominates but it is not intact. Some earlier single storey dwellings, e.g. **30** and **32 High Barholm** (c. 1800 and c. 1787), have kept their swept dormers in slate and timber. Other buildings are later infill, higher to the eaves, harder on the jamb. The most obvious exception, foil to the rule, is

D **The Trust Inn** (1903) at 8 Low Barholm, designed by J. Craig Barr; a Tudorised pub sited at a corner break in the street wall. And, endearingly tucked in at the end of the street, **The Sweet Shop**, quaintly dilapidated, an absurdly low two-storey one-room-wide property sporting its debased Palladian window at first

E floor. Elbowing against The Sweet Shop is **21 High Barholm** (1908-09) a well cut three-storey tenement by Peter Caldwell. The road bends and, as Barn Green bypass cuts left breaching the sense of enclosure, there is suddenly too much space. Ewing Street restores containment as it climbs uphill to Steeple Square, the left hand side a consistent two-storey scale: at first, relatively recent housing, windows too wide, mouldings too proud; latterly some older properties — **2-4 Ewing Street** (c. 1810) very plain but very good. The right hand side, crow-stepping here and there, is more mixed, almost the best thing on offer being the whin walls that swing up into Well Road.

Renfrew District

Carson & Hunter

Renfrew District

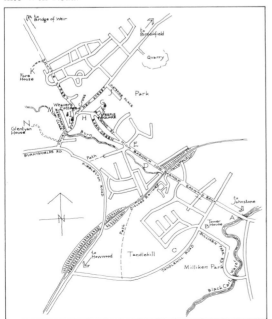

Top 34 High Barholm.
Middle The Trust Inn.
Above 2-4 Ewing Street.

Above View towards Steeple Square in Victorian times. **Right** Steeple Building.

F **Steeple Building**
David Kerr (1755, rebuilt 1782)
A local master mason designed this isolated two-storeyed piended block to house both school and meal market, fronting it with the high square tower that dominates the village skyline. Half-way up the tower, a bronze statue (1923) of the village's legendary piper Habbie Simpson (*a contemporary of Shakespeare*, notes one writer mustering all the spurious association of local pride) stands in the central niche of a tripartite Palladian feature. Above, the squat stone spire that tops off the tower has something of the flavour of a provincial Venetian Romanesque church. But it is all stoutly Scottish in a robust parochial way.

East Church.

G **East Church**
James Brown (1787-89)
Built for a relief congregation this austere rubble-walled kirk was consciously modelled on Castlehead Church, Paisley (*q.v.*). Brown, *from whom the site had been obtained*, produced a high plain symmetrical building with dressed margins and quoins, round arched windows and a piended roof. In 1855 a new ceiling was installed and in 1859 the bow-fronted session house and vestry were altered and improved. Extensive internal reshaping (1872-73) by Robert Baldie.

RCAHMS

The Cross before demolitions.

Two origins of the name Kilbarchan have been suggested. Both accept the common explanation for the prefix "kil" meaning "cell" or "church", but whereas one proposes its addition to the name of Barchan, a late 6th century Celtic priest who settled in the area, the other prefers a second Gaelic derivation from the words "bar", a brae, and "chan", a vale; certainly a valid description of the local topography.

Steeple Street

The Cross, so evidently once the heart of the village, has been ill served by the depredations of road engineers whose obsessions with sight lines have, ironically, blinded them to those qualities of place now only to be seen in old photographs and prints. Picking up the street line excised by Barn Green, **16 Steeple Street** (late 19th century) turns a crisp eaves cornice obliquely into a narrow yard leading to the **Old Manse** (c. 1730). Modest, like the weaving shed which abuts it, the manse may well be in part a reconstruction of an earlier 17th century house. Across the yard **8-10 Steeple Street** (1835), recalls the spirit of Low and High Barholm — though here entrance and frontal chimney stack, have been curved round the corner. **2-4 Steeple Street** (c. 1760) faces The Cross with some grandeur despite its later top storey.

Renfrew District

Above The Old Manse off Steeple Street.
Left 3-10 Steeple Street.

Renfrew District

Renfrew District

Walker

Above Weaver's Cottage now in care of National Trust for Scotland.
Right Lintel inscription at Weaver's Cottage.

Various tools *and artefacts of the weaver's craft, including a 200-year-old loom which still functions, are preserved in the weaver's cottage honouring the huge part which weaving has played in Kilbarchan life for two and a half centuries. From 1695, when there were perhaps 30 or 40 looms, the industry expanded rapidly until almost a century later, some 800 looms, mostly hand operated, could be found at work in the ground floor room of almost every house in the village. Such cottage-based industry never produced vast profits and Kilbarchan remained something of a rural backwater; on the other hand, it did not entail over specialisation so that while later recessions tore deep into the fabric of Paisley's textile industry, Kilbarchan's varied production of tartans, ponchos, repp shawls, druggets, scarves, etc. could be maintained throughout the 1800s and well into the present century.*

Weaver's Cottage
(1723)
Erected, as the inscription over the entrance records, *anno 1723 by Andrew Brydein, John Brydein, Jenat Brydein* and looking prim and well-scrubbed as restored National Trust properties do, this relatively small split-level rubble building is nevertheless of great interest. Typically part workshop and part dwelling it presents a delightfully random facade to the sloping western side of The Cross. Another inscription, in equally finely cut 18th century letters, can be found on a marriage lintel in the south gable. In the garden are a bee-bole, a knocking stane and a mysterious stone head known as the Idol. In the northern single-storey half of the cottage is a rare original example of cruck roofing.

New Street has lost its original character but **Gateside Place** is remarkably intact: two-storey 1830s housing all similar yet all varied, a little prettified by pastel painting, it retains some interesting properties. **5 Shuttle Street** (c. 1780) was formerly a weaving shop with its attic dwelling above; **9** (c. 1800), two-storeyed and crow-stepped, stands derelict; **Well Cottage**, single-storeyed with swept timber dormers, boasts a problematical 1702 date.

RCAHMS

Right Gateside Place.

K Fore House
(1773)
Built by the Barbour family who, from being
candlemakers, had turned to the increasingly profitable
business of linen bleaching, it testifies, like many
another house in the county, to cultural aspiration and
gracious living paid for by the booming textile trade.
It sits on a low basement, a three-window-wide
Georgian mansion of orthodox but elegant disposition,
the only jarring accents being the small console
brackets clinging to either end of the facade pediment.

Toonfit
Church Street, winding downhill to the oldest part
of the village, has a couthy intimacy found perhaps
nowhere else in Renfrewshire. This is not so much
the consequence of distinctive building, since the
houses packed together to form the left hand wall of
the street are of widely varying date and differing
scale, but somehow the narrowness of the street, its
absence of pavements, the way it cuts below the level
of the church graveyard and curves down into the
trees, all combine to create something, or rather some
place, special. Fortunately, the rough red sandstone
Gothic bulk of William H. Howie's **West Church**
(1899-1901), threatens but does not command the
scene.

L Old Parish Church
James Baird (1724)
Its figure is that of a St George's Cross, the body of
the church standing east and west; and there is an
aisle on the north, which has belonged to the family of
Craigends, and was not even taken down when the
rest of the church was built anew.
This new church of 1724 is a roughcast rubble-built
structure with dressed surrounds, quoins and four
crow-stepped gables, one of which was given an ogee-
capped stone bellcote *after the pattern of the one at*
Port Glasgow. Further work in 1792 produced a
detached session house (demolished 1899) and
churchyard gates, the piers of which still stand. In
1858 Alexander Kirkland carried out several
alterations which included placing a balustraded
square entrance tower in the north-east corner of the
church.

Top Fore House.
Middle Church Street dipping
past the Old Parish Church to
Toonfit.
Above Old Parish Church; 19th
century entrance tower.

Fountain Memorial to the poet
Robert Allan.

*Robert Allan, one of many weaver-
poets, viewed his literary craft with
cynical pathos:*

"The poet, madly bent on fame,
  Wi' stringing rhymes an' blether,
*Aye crazed wi' care, or crossed in
  love,*
  Ill fated a' thegither,
*Still, still he twines his wreath of
  hope*
  An' is the vera slave o't —
*But what's to him a deathless
  name,*
  When he gets but a grave o't?"

Right Merchants' Close.
Below Glentyan House.

Merchants' Close still exists as a quiet
residential *cul-de-sac* ending in **Woodside** (c. 1800) a
plain two-storey door-in-the-middle gabled house.
What was once Cow Loan remains as a prolongation
of Church Street (note the **Allan Fountain**); but
there are no weavers' rows, only high whin walls
channelling the road up through the thickly wooded
estate to open country on the west and south.

Glentyan House
(1781-95)

A two-storey and basement Georgian house, five bays
in width, the central three of which are pedimented
and project lightly on the main east front. The north
and south gables also have central pediments each
rising between twinned chimney stacks. During the
19th century extensive additions were made to the
west. Without doubt Kilbarchan's finest house, yet,
though built by Alexander Spiers with the wealth the
village created, it seems now to live its life remote
from the community, hidden, aloof and inaccessible.

HOWWOOD

The road from Johnstone to Howwood parallels the
railway and the course of the Black Cart.
Midtownfield Bleachworks (1835-40) lie to the
south; a 37 foot water wheel has gone, but some of
the 19th century buildings remain, adapted to the
needs of the electronics industry. At the edge of the
wood stands **Tor Bracken** (c. 1898) a large half-
timbered tile-hung verandahed house; in the grounds,
a vast gabled stables block, equally Tudorised but
implacably symmetrical, and an octagonal summer
house on rustic tree-trunk columns.

Howwood itself — *Hollow Wood*, as Groome's
Gazetteer still referred to it in 1883 — has little to
offer. **9-10 George Street**, a continuous run of one-
and two-storey rubble houses, is all that remains of the
village's oldest street. **The Inn** (c. 1770), is a two-
storey-and-attic house with restored astragals,
pleasantly painted margins, and, on each side, gabled
single-storey wings that once served as shops.
Wellbank (c. 1885), a cottage villa, is distinguished
by peaked gablets on the attic bays, ornamental
bargeboards, and shaped margins to its tripartite
windows.

Elliston Farm (c. 1800) single-storey and attic,
debased Palladian windows flanking a central flat-
pedimented doorpiece, is the first of a series of farms
and steadings dotted along the higher ground south of

The Inn, Howwood; formerly The
County Hotel.

Renfrew District

Castle Semple Loch. Past **Elliston Castle**, a 15th century tower house reduced to a high crumbling stand of ivy-covered wall, comes **East Gavin** (c. 1780) gabled, with scroll skew putts; then the clusterd buildings of **Mid Gavin**, 18th century in origin but now much engulfed in polychromatic brickwork. **Low Belltrees** (c. 1740), on Cuppleton Brae, is more austere and Scottish, crow-stepped with a pedimented Renaissance doorpiece in rough vein.

Newton of Belltrees village, drawn by the author.

Newton of Belltrees
A delightful hamlet consisting of a short hillside street of mainly late 18th century houses, rubble-built with some stone dressings; unexceptional individually but amiable in the group.

Auchengrange
(c. 1832)
Formerly Wattieston, what remains after the demolition of various Victorian additions to the original two-storey Georgian house is not quite right, but the overall scale is good, the wide porch rather special with its Corinthian columns and heavy timbered roof, and the stables yard attractively irregular with their touch of Gothick whimsy.

Lochside.

Lochside
(1771)
Submerged in this strange pile, not far from the edge of Castle Semple Loch, is the original three-bay L-plan house built by the Caldwell family who lived at Lochsyde throughout the 18th century. It is clearly revealed by the single-light sash-and-case windows at ground and first floor, skewputts at second floor and the outline of the old skews on the raised east gable. The unfortunate additions of the third storey and the three-storey wing to the west were designed in 1909 by J. R. Johnstone of Troon although it was not until 1925 that Johnstone and T. Harold Hughes carried out the work. Perhaps due restoration can yet be made.

Building Pictures

RCAHMS

CASTLE SEMPLE

Castle Semple House in 1907.

Castle Semple House

(1735-40) demolished

Today's visitor will find nothing of the mansion that Colonel William McDowall built for himself on the north-west side of Castle Semple Loch. Demolishing the medieval *Castle Semple, the principal messwage (*sic*) of a fair lordship of the same denomination,* he constructed a new, provincially Palladian, house with a double rank of flanking outbuildings. Not content with this, the McDowalls obtained plans from Robert Adam (1791) which would have transformed the house with all the towered and battlemented conceits of romantic classicism. These ambitious proposals were, however, never executed. The fortunes of the McDowalls started to wane and in 1808 the sale of the estate lands was begun, the largest portion, including the mansion, passing into the hands of the Harvey family in 1813. After a promising start, the Harveys found the burden too great and the condition of buildings and policies deteriorated throughout the Victorian era. In the 20th century disintegration accelerated and finally, in the 1960s, Castle Semple was razed save for a quirky and incongruous house conversion of its easternmost wing.

McDowall's mansion stood on the northern shore of the loch close to its outflow as the Black Cart Water. From the west, it was approached through the

Robert Adam's re-modelled facade for Castle Semple House.

RCAHMS/Soane Museum

RCAHMS

Rae

RCAHMS

Top West Gates and Lodge.
Above Stables Block.
Above Garthland Bridge.
Below Collegiate Church.

West Gates at Lochwinnoch (*q.v.*) and down a long drive that ran between extensive estate plantations and loch side. From the north, a track passed over the hill through the home farm. Remains of the walled garden can be found; there is a **Farmhouse** (c. 1800) with a Doric porch; and a long **Stables Block** (c. 1770), part ashlar part rubble, with Gothicized end pavilions, which has recently (1985) been quietly converted to residential use by David Rae. From the east, the mansion could be reached across **Garthland Bridge** (1767) at Howwood, through the castellated Gothic of the **East Gates** (demolished) and down a long avenue by the riverside. Here McDowall created the estate's deer park, building a little octagonal folly, the so-called **Temple** (c. 1770), on the summit of Kenmure Hill. Silhouetted on the skyline for miles around, it is roofless and crumbling now; a forlorn place in which it is hard to imagine the laird's guests gathered around the fireplace looking out on the chase below. Crossing St Bride's Burn by **Fancy Bridge** (c. 1740), the visitor would at length enter the wide forecourt of the great house.

The Peel
(c. 1550)
One of the two relics from the medieval demesne, this low tower was built on the southern margin of the loch, close to Lochside, perhaps for defence (its site was originally an island). Latterly it was used, as Crawfurd puts it, *when the family of Sempill did recreate themselves by diversion in their boat of pleasure on the lake.*

Collegiate Church
(1504-05)
Less reduced than the Peel this roofless building, erected above the north end of the loch close to the site of the ancient castle stands to the wall-head, a long rectangular chapel with a square tower at one end and semi-octagonal apse at the other. Recessed in the chancel wall is the elaborately designed cusped tomb (c. 1515) of the founder, John, first Lord Sempill.

Renfrew District

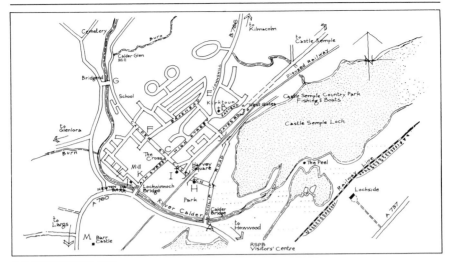

LOCHWINNOCH

While the Black Cart Water flows out of one end of
Castle Semple Loch, the River Calder flows *in* at the
other. Released from a steep valley, where its
tumbling course once powered a series of grain and
cotton mills, the Calder takes a long sweep to the east
filtering through marshland before it enters the
shallow loch from the south. Here the village of
Lochwinnoch grew, stretching across the haugh lands
from the river to the kirk. At one end are the bridges,
linking the village with the east-west route that
traverses the neck of drained land separating Castle
A Semple Loch from Barr Loch — **Calder Bridge**
(c. 1790), formerly New Bridge, a gently humped
stone structure of three segmental arches on wide
cutwater plinths, and, leading directly into Main
Street, **Lochwinnoch Bridge**, an iron bridge (1902)
built to replace the old Calderhaugh Brig. At the other
end where the ground begins to rise on Johnshill, is
the Auld Kirktoun clustered around graveyard and
church — or what's left of it.

B **St Winnoc's Church**
Demolition in the early 19th century spared little
more than the crow-stepped front gable of the old
cross-planned kirk, once a *notable gospel shop.* One
narrow room in depth, this rump gable was retained
as a watch tower to guard the graves from *the
depradations* (sic) *of the resurrectionists.* Auld Simon the
villagers call it, perhaps after the local weaver who
used to keep its clock wound and working. It looks
more like a mausoleum now, but still carries its four-
columned open bellcote with entablature and ogee cap
surmounted by a weather vane in the form of a
plough.

Auld Simon: the rump of St
Winnoc's Church.

Renfrew District

High Street looking towards Kirktoun.

The Cross; Cross House at the corner of Main Street and Church Street.

C The Cross

Lochwinnoch's plan (1788) follows the pattern of the cross, each of its four streets still retaining something of the original single- or two-storey gable-to-gable character. Writing in 1831, Crawfurd records that *the plan of the village was the late Garthland's,* i.e. it was the creation of the local laird, William McDowall of Garthland and Castle-Semple (1749-1810). Control on architectural development focused at **The Cross** itself where *Garthland's plan seems to require some ornamental form . . .* Two-storey buildings on three of the four corners are more or less intact. The **Royal Bank** has a leaded dome over a corner entrance and segmentally pedimented dormers left and right of its gabled High Street facade. The remaining two properties, symmetrically related, both have gables to Church Street which bend down in curved skews around the corner. **Cross House** (c. 1819) is the better, not least because of a surprising Corinthian-columned doorpiece with an odd stilted lintel.

High Street

There is a modest tarnished dignity: **10-12** (c. 1790) is very low, single-storey rubble with dressed surrounds to small windows almost square in proportion; **18-22** (c. 1810) has a single second floor window in the central pedimented spread below its street front chimney; **29** (c. 1810), similar but without the attic window, has a pilastered doorpiece; **31** (c. 1810), however, boasts two windows lighting a third storey tucked in behind a chimneyed gable front.

D   The **Library and Museum** (1857) incorporates what was once the local school, *Erected by Colonel D. H. McDowall of Garthland*, a low sandstone building whose gable skews simulate overlapping tiles. **46-66 High Street** (1983-84), is a stretch of infill sheltered housing cleverly and successfully designed by Renfrew District Council architects to reinforce the existing streetscape, varying eaves height, jamb detail and colour. At **St Winnoc Road** the straight line wall of High Street comes to an end in the broad swept pediment of **The Corner** public house (c. 1820).

Kirktoun

Eastend has had the doorways and window openings of its original houses swallowed up like tombstones in graveyard or garden walls. **Johnshill** still retains a few early properties built hard to the street. **5** (c. 1780) is a low two-storey rubble house with crow-stepped gables. Similar, but larger with plain skews

E   terminating in huge scroll skew-putts, **19** (c. 1780) has an attractively irregular front. A stable pend penetrates the building at the higher northern end (1825) so that the house must be approached by a two-sided forestair in the pavement width. **Crookside** is grander by virtue of its siting, scale and outbuildings.

Calder Street

31-33 is tidy, a rusticated mid-Victorian terrace with chamfered rybats; and **35-37** (c. 1810), merits a second glance, though its charm is a little compromised by neglect. To the right, the street wall has been maintained, with a few creditable Victorian

F   contributions. Half way up is **Braevar** (c. 1820), an austere villa with tall tripartite windows on both floors. Nearby is **Westdene** (c. 1830), the former Free Church Manse, a delightful Georgian mansion, plain white, crisp and elegant — certainly one of Crawfurd's *good houses*. **36-40 Calder Street** step demurely along the street slope only to be dwarfed by what follows — at **46-50** an unexpected tenement rearing its massive rusticated wall along the crest of the hill. Here, a look back through the heart of the village below terminates in the low tower of the Calder United Free Church (*q.v.*).

Calder Glen

Past the **Public School** (1905), School Board symmetrical in red sandstone by Charles Davidson, lies the beautiful wooded valley of Calder Glen. It begins at Bridgend, the earliest crossing of the Calder

Top 46-66 High Street infill housing.
Above 19 Johnshill.

36-50 Calder Street.

Top Bridgend and Bow Bridge.
Above Calder U.F. Church.

St John's Parish Church

connecting Kirktoun with the route past Barr to Glen
G Garnock and Largs. The balustered **Bow Bridge**
dates back to the 17th century although its present
form results from improvement and widening in 1814.
Across the bridge are three ancient cottages all *restored
beyond recognition* but with a marriage stone on the
westernmost gable recording the date 1696. Behind
these three the river pours over the Falls constructed
in 1787 when a lade was run to serve the Calderpark
Mill (1788, destroyed 1874) on Calder Street. Part of
the three-storey **Calder Mill** (1814), has been
converted into a house; but **Calderbank
Bleachworks** are in ruins. **Fallside**, for all the world
like the modest 1830s mansion of some local
millowner, is the brilliant conceit and deceit of Noad
and Wallace, who designed it in 1958!

Church Street
H **Calder U.F. Church** (1792), terminating the axis from
The Cross, exerts a sense of some grander design.
The church began as a Burghers' Chapel, octagonal in
plan, rubble-built with dressed margins. It was the
intention of the Burghers' patron, William McDowall,
to raise a steeple in front but he *desisted from his
original plan, for he found the sect all almost democrats.*
The task was not completed until 1815 when Harvey
of Castle-Semple, the new laird, built a low
battlemented and turretted tower on McDowall's
stickit steeple. In 1866 the interior was completely
recast. Hidden behind is the **Manse** (1825) a tidy
gabled house with a consoled doorpiece in front and
turnpike stair at the rear.

Harvey Square
Lying between the U.F. Church and The Cross, the
square introduced a powerful additional element in the
village townscape. Garthland's original plan envisaged
a small square opening out symmetrically on each side
of Church Street just before the Burghers' Chapel was
I reached, but the decision was soon made to build **St
John's Parish Church** (1806-08) on the south-
western side of this formal space. The new church,
octagonal like its neighbour but considerably elongated
in plan and superior in architectural conception and
detail, was built by *one Andrew from Kilbarchan, a
mason*, who went bankrupt during its construction.
Nonetheless, the work was finished, including the
expensive ashlar steeple which rises from a splendid
Doric porch, to a pilastered belfry, clock, and obelisk
spire.
   The Square, only half the size first planned, was
still spacious enough to be *useful for markets for cattle,
shows, reform hustings, etc.* Though it lacks strong
architectural definition, there *are* three detached two-

storey houses built in deliberately formal relationship. The **Square House** (c. 1810) with full height end pilasters, and an Ionic doorpiece, **Novar** (c. 1810) which has the same pilasters and cornice, but a Tuscan porch and later ground floor bays, and **Armannoch** (c. 1810) similar, but with only the plainest details. The last two flank the entrance to Harvey Terrace, a long axial route running from the church to Gates Road and the great **West Gates** (c. 1770) of Castle-Semple estate, a castellated triple-arched open portal, badly marred by lodge house conversions, but full of Gothic fun.

J

Square House, Harvey Square.

Main Street
The fourth arm of The Cross, extends the line of High Street to the river. **Calderhaugh Mill** (1789), a four-storey-and-attic gabled building with a lower engine and boiler house, is almost all that is left of a much larger development where cotton and later silk were spun. Beside it, **Calderhaugh House** (c. 1780), a gabled mansion with portholed pediment, doorpiece and extra large scrolled skew-putts, looks across its lawn to the riverside. Opposite the Mill, **Calder House** (c. 1820) is a large, but fairly straightforward, two-storey-and-basement house enhanced by a timber porch with fluted Ionic pilasters, but marred by three large hipped dormers. Two gateways are flanked by pinnacled cluster piers. Across the Calder, to the right, is **Newton of Barr**, a short straight stretch of mainly single-storey houses, part of Garthland's original conception.

K

L

With an acid sense *of social status, Crawfurd in his* Cairn of Lochwinyoch Matters *(1827-37) remarks that "In general, the houses of this village are very plain. They have a* raw *appearance or mean, as suitable for weavers and cotton spinners [although there are] eleven good houses for the respectable inhabitants, such as professional men, managers of the cotton mills, retired manufacturers and merchants, etc. . . . all almost* [sic] *of two stories, embellished with statuary and flowers round them."*

Calderhaugh House.

Renfrew District

Renfrew District

Barr Castle.

Renfrew District

M **Barr Castle**
(16th century)
The antiquity of the lands of Barr, which lie just
beyond this south-western edge of Lochwinnoch, is
stoutly attested in the tower-house of **Barr Castle**.
Standing by a wooded rise above Barr Loch, the keep
has been well preserved, though its corbelled
battlements and four corner turrets are no longer
roofed, and outbuildings, which once formed a small
courtyard, have vanished. Several inscriptions carrying
initials or dates can be found.

Garthland House
(from c. 1800)
Known as Garpel and later as Barr House, it was built
by David King but later extended (c. 1820-30) by
William McDowall of Garthland (1770-1840). These
additions, elongating the main gabled block on the
north, were sympathic to the original *British* mix of
Scottish 17th century dormers and tall Tudor chimney
shafts — although a slight, vaguely disturbing change
in overall scale was introduced. A Victorian porch and
castellated bay window continued this trend.

Glenlora
(c. 1840)
A mile to the west on rising ground above Corsefield
Road this asymmetrical ashlar house has been carried
out in an unconventional but suitably provincial
Tuscan idiom with twin-columned porch, widespread
eaves, and pedimented attic tower.

LINWOOD

At Elderslie, road and rail branch north-west towards Gryffeside, the road passing through a giant car plant to reach Linwood. The production lines are idle now, like most of Linwood's dependent population. Not for the first time this industrial village has grown only to find fickle fortune in economic specialisation. Robertson, writing in 1818, described

> . . . *a regular built town on a handsome plan . . . it has arisen entirely from a cotton work erected about 30 years ago, of an immense size, calculated to work 25,000 spindles, and, when completed, to employ 1,800 people.*

There is nothing handsome about Linwood now — if, in truth, there ever was. The Linwood mill, 1794, which was *the most splendid establishment in the cotton spinning business perhaps in Britain,* is no more, the sad fate of its cotton workers repeated in another single industrial development of even more *immense size.* What remains is a derelict car plant, and a place which is neither town nor village but one bleak, successively enlarged, housing estate.

Clippens, a plain, two-storey-and-basement mansion of c. 1820 has a flying staircase rising to a simple Doric doorpiece. The house has been boarded up; although, in the basement, its future has been somewhat invidiously assured as a centre of administrative control in the event of nuclear attack.

Clippens House.

Victoria Road.

Walker

BROOKFIELD

The A761 between Linwood and Brookfield begins and ends with a hospital. First, there is **Johnstone Combination Hospital**, begun 1887 to a design submitted in competition by John Woodrow, extended 1897 by Cowan and Watson, a motley collection of unremarkable stone and brick buildings of differing dates. **Merchiston Hospital** (built 1880, demolished 1985) was purchased in 1948 by the local health authority as a home for the mentally handicapped. Now, a settlement of sheltered accommodation, designed by Scottish Health Service architects, has spread eastwards in a series of rurally white walls and intersecting monopitch blocks.

Brookfield extends north from the road to the railway — a pleasant suburban island. **Victoria Road** has a group of four semi-detached rough-cast cottages (c. 1899-1900) built by the South Western Property Co. to a design by Watson and Salmond — an unexpected intimation of Hampstead Garden Suburb.

South of the road is the rump of the estate of the barony of Johnstone acquired by the Houstoun family during the reign of Charles I. Sold in 1733, the estate took the name of its new owner, James Milliken, a wealthy sugar baron who, demolishing the Houstouns' house, built himself *a large three-storey mansion*. A century later this was destroyed by fire and in 1836 replaced by a long plain two-storey-and-basement mansion-house *in Grecian style*. In 1887-88 the estate was bought by a Paisley starch manufacturer, Archibald Mackenzie, and in 1921 it became the property of the architect George Boswell. Boswell demolished Milliken House and proceeded to create a smaller dwelling from the estate factor's house, stables and cartshed.

The White House of Milliken is thus a conversion carried out by Boswell in the 1920s and by Boswell, Mitchell & Johnston in 1953. The more classical east front, three widely-spaced windows wide, has a central pedimented block with pavilion roof, on either side of which are the pedimented gables of the former outbuildings. To the west, around a flagged court, ground floor extensions project to create new rooms and a bowed entrance hall. Just outside the courtyard is a laughing stone gnome statue of the Kilbarchan piper, Habbie Simpson, and down the drive to the south a roofless **Doocot**.

White House of Milliken.

Walker

RCAHMS

HOUSTON

A **Crosslee Mill**

Crosslee Mill (1793), a short walk east from Bridge of Weir, between the Gryffe and the overgrown mill lade, was the biggest on the river, a six-storey spinning mill employing about three hundred workers. Nothing remains. In 1916-17, however, a remarkable reinforced concrete factory for spinning cordite fuses took its place. The building, by William D. McLennan, had a two-storey wide-span rib-and-panel structure, glazed between columns; altogether astonishingly *modern* in such a rural spot.

North of Crosslee lies the 18th century planned village of Houston. Houston, i.e. *Hew's toun*, was the name attached to the few dwellings which in the 13th century had clustered around the castle of Hugo de Kilpeter. In due course, place and family shared the

South Street looking east; Mercat Cross in the foreground.

Crosslee Mill (dem. 1986).

Walker

South Street looking west.

St Fillan died in 649 somewhere west of Loch Earn. His arm was preserved some 700 years as a relic. In a silver shrine it was carried at the head of King Robert the Bruce's army at Bannockburn.

same name. Castle and village altered little until, in 1740, the estate passed into more enterprising hands. In 1781 the castle was partially demolished and a New Town of thirty-five houses was begun.

> *Six of the houses are two-storeys high, and two of them are slated; many of them contain two families, or one family and a shop for looms . . . The new village of Houston is neatly built; the front walls are of hewn stone from the mansion house and tower of Houston.*

North Street runs west from the original settlement at the castle gates with South Street parallel on the other side of the Houston Burn. The north side of North Street retains some of its original gable-to-gable character: at one end **Houston Inn** (1784), a plain two-storey house much traduced by rear extensions; at the other, **Houston Cottage** (1829), by local builders King, a cottage villa with curved attic dormers, a wide doorway with tall side-lights and consoles, and gate piers bearing elongated lancet motifs.

South Street is broader but more defined, with its west end intact: **Cochrane Place**, dated 1781, has been ill served by the elongation of its first floor windows into dormers; charmingly proportioned, however, are **Kilmory** and **Lamorna** (c. 1800), adjacent single-storey dwellings with central chimneyed gables. The **Mercat Cross** has a sundial headpiece dated 1713 and a tail chamfered shaft which may be of 14th century origin. Nearby is **The Fox and Hounds** (c. 1820) another plain pub created from three separate houses. As the writer of the Second Statistical Account remarked in 1836:

> *Inns — These are numerous, and their effects obvious.*

Barrfield, a long symmetrical cottage on Main Street, harled with dressed margins, is early 19th century. The **Free Church** is grey and austere to a fault. **Houston School** (1911-12) by William Kerr of Alloa architects John Melvin and Son, has a two-storey red sandstone symmetrical front with dentilled eaves course, scroll carving around the windows above Boys' and Girls' entrances, and a domed roof ventilator with corner columns.

St Fillan's Church (1841), at Fourwindings, is a severe chapel with gable belfry. It was once the only place of worship for the entire Roman Catholic population between Paisley and Port Glasgow. A low presbytery and a disproportionately high school building (1872) adjoin the church. To the west, by

Strathclyde Region

South Mound, is **Gryffe High School** (1978-79) by Strathclyde Region architects, an exciting multi-coloured ship of a building approached with some flair along a concrete red-railed gangway.

B **Houston and Killellan Church**
David Thomson (1874-75)
Lying at the older eastern end of the village, by the gates of Houston House, its plain Gothic Revival with low castellated tower and simple slated spire replaced an earlier 18th century church. In the graveyard are the **Monteath Tomb** (1828) and some exquisitely incised 18th and 19th century stones and slabs. In the church itself is a 15th century sepulchral monument to Sir Partick Houston of that Ilk *under a canopy of free stone, with the effigies of himself and his lady, as big as the life.*

C **Houston House**
(from 17th century)
Part may even be 16th century but the grandeur is all Victorian swagger. In 1872, a new mansion was constructed south-east of the older work and in 1893-95 more extensive additions to the west and east were built to designs by David Thomson. Thomson's Baronial gathers the disparate pieces into a picturesque composition that culminates in a 77 feet tower rising above the entrance to give views out over the estate trees.

Killellan
D The ruins of **St Fillan's Church** can be found at Killellan (Kil'illan — the cell of Fillan) halfway across the hill to Kilmacolm. Its simple rectangular form is

Renfrew District

Top Gryffe High School.
Above Houston and Killellan Church.

St Fillan's Church; ruined walls seen across graveyard.

Renfrew District

F

Renfrew District

that of *the familiar, unadorned Reformation edifice,* though hereabouts there has been a place of worship since the 8th century. On the south wall are some weathered memorial fragments, a 17th century inscribed tablet and a lintel date of 1635. **Killellan Manse**, hard by, is rubble-built with corbie-steps and a turnpike stair. Parts may date from the 17th century but the building has been repeatedly recast and restored: in 1783, in 1927 by A. T. Balfour Paul and in 1963 by R. Mervyn Noad. So secluded and bosky is the grouping of church, manse and kirkyard it is easy to pass by this ancient romantic place. **St Peter's Well**, a medieval water source once thought to possess miraculous powers, now bubbles beneath what looks like nothing so much as a stone dog kennel at the foot of a field behind Greenhill Farm.

RCAHMS

Top Killellan Manse.
Above Craigends House; watercolour by David Bryce.

Much more spectacularly Baronial, especially in its high turretted gable arching over the main entrance, was **Craigends**, *perhaps David Bryce's greatest country house. Built in 1857 for the Cunninghames whose lands lay on the south side of the Gryffe, it was demolished in 1967 to make way for the tracts of private housing which have since eaten up much of the open country between Houston and Crosslee.*

F **Barochan House**
(from 17th century)
The ancient seat of the Flemings, *on a craggie hill, well sheltered among its ancient woods* is mostly modern (1896) Arts and Crafts Baronial. Further reduced by demolition in 1947, it still incorporates 17th century work in a high crow-stepped gable obliquely set to the north-east.

BRIDGE OF WEIR

Bridge of Weir is a divided village: divided not by the river Gryffe which, passing over its salmon weir, bends behind and below Main Street in a deep, industrially cluttered cut, but by the railway. Trains no longer run, but the divide, physical and social, remains. Approaching from the east, you sense it immediately. The road parallels the tracks, passes the harled Toy-Town-towered church of **St Mary the Virgin** (1909), by Thomas Dykes and Dale, and then, in a sudden chicane, bridges the derelict line into Main Street.

G

At this point there is a choice. Uphill, Ranfurly: villa-land. Across the bridge, between railway and river: the village. Neither is very old. But while the village owes its origin to the cotton mills that grew up on Gryffeside from 1790s to 1840s, Ranfurly is the more recent creation of the railway.

The approach up to Ranfurly is guarded by the twin bastions of Victorian respectability: church and bank. **St Machar's Church** (1877-78), by Lewis Shanks, brother of one of the local millowners, is early Gothic; a raised nave with four gabled bays to the north. A delightful approach, passes through the lych gate (1939) and beneath the trees. A chancel, brick faced internally, with a small hall below was, added in 1909-10 by Alexander Hislop. The **Clydesdale Bank** (1908), Baird & Thomson, is as securely suburban as a square-cut two-storey villa can be.

H **Castle Terrace**
(formerly the Ranfurly Hotel) Robert R. Raeburn (1882)

A line first reached Bridge of Weir from Johnstone in 1864 and, a few years later, the mansions of commuting Glasgow businessmen, tempted by clean air and railway discount, began to appear.
In 1871 "The Greenock & Ayrshire Railway Co." made it known that they would confer a privilege to those building a house in Bridge of Weir, by granting annually tickets at half their season ticket prices for a period of seven years . . . for the convenience of intending house builders a copy of the Ranfurly feu charter could be seen at Bridge of Weir railway station.

Ranfurly Hotel, now Castle Terrace.

Paisley Museum

Walker

Top Ranfurly Hotel; original prospectus.
Above Easterhill.
Below Beauly, formerly Redlands, drawn by Alexander McGibbon.

Built by the Bonars, proprietors of Ranfurly Estate, vicissitudes of function have attended the terrace's history — hotel, refugee centre, auxiliary hospital, private school, flats and shops. Its asymmetrical Baronial implosion of all the Bryce-derived bits — cross-stepped gables, bartizans, corbelled stacks, rough and smooth masonry, off-centre Frenchified tower (still with its wrought iron skyline) — stands as an elongated castellated portal defending the salubrious slopes above. The original design was brilliantly and *invisibly* extended eastwards by James Miller in 1901.

A climb up the 155 steps that rise in the shadow of Castle Terrace's west gable exhausts the body and humbles the spirit. Is this part of the plan? This is rich man's country and no mistake. The roads are generous, the feus large, and the houses, old and new, redolent of commercial and professional success.

Beauly (1898-99) (formerly Redlands), Hazelwood Road, is a red sand-stone L-plan villa by Honeyman & Keppie. Arrangement and details are generally Keppie but not so the semi-circular stair tower tucked close to the entrance. Its conical roof, wide eaves, vertical leaded-light windows and the stiffly *Art Nouveau* carving of the baluster panels all suggest the experimental meddling of Charles Rennie Mackintosh. At **Easterhill** (1902-03), Bankhead Road, the same frustrated inventiveness emerges through Keppie's control, this time in the harled walls, window grouping and characteristic dormers found more familiarly at Mackintosh's contemporary Hill House, Helensburgh.

Renfrew District

Brannochlie, Prieston Road, is the elaboration of an old farmhouse; **The Cairn** is grander, combining stone crow-stepping and dressings with roughcast walls; **The Homestead**, Golf Course Road has a two-gable Voysey front: all are in the early 1900s austere mode of John A. Campbell. Between 1904 and 1908, Campbell built five of the houses on Golf Course Road, the impetus coming from his commission to design **Ranfurly Castle Golf Clubhouse** (1904-05) when the club moved to its Clevans course. The Clubhouse is a magnificent four-storeys, a castle indeed — even without its unbuilt clocktower! Brick below, white roughcast and black half-timbering above, its texture of astragalled windows has been cruelly interrupted by some philistine changes to the glazing.

    Ranfurly Castle itself is barely to be seen. Hidden in a copse on the old golf course, the small keep, raised by the Knoxes in the early 15th century, is as MacGibbon & Ross described it a century ago, *rent and ruinous.*

Barnbeth

W. G. Rowan (1914)

Built with shipping money this rural mansion lies beyond the golf courses. Through the iron gates (a combined gate pier and doocot still tenanted by white doves) the drive passes motor house, outbuildings, well and sun-dial to reach the hefty timber porch. The house is a long two-storeyed roughcast building enlivened by brick trim. But the gardens are its supreme delight and no place more perfect to dream away a summer afternoon than the balcony of the half-peristyled gazebo which pokes its ogee roof above the hedges.

The very name of Knox *is enough to stir the imagination of local Reformist zeal. One of Paisley's lesser poets, "On Viewing Ranfurly Castle by Moonlight", was moved to write:*

> *"Thou venerable pile, whose walls proclaim*
> *Departed greatness and a fair domain;*
>
> . . .
>
> *But Knox, who hath been fam'd in every age,*
> *Revered as a scholar, well known as a sage;*
> *The power of Papal Rome he did pull down,*
> *And snatched a jewel from St Peter's crown.*
>
> . . .
>
> *For ages here his ancestors did reside —*
> *Here, for three hundred years, they did abide . . ."*

Doggerel delusion! In fact, though Knox did visit Finlaystone (q.v.), it was a distant collateral branch of the family who lived at Ranfurly.

Above Brannochlie, Prieston Road.
Below Barnbeth.

Renfrew District

Top Lintwhite School.
Middle Freeland Church.
Above Gryffe Viaduct.

Lintwhite School

James Miller (1900)

Surely one of Miller's best works. In what he called his *domestic style of architecture* — apt enough description for the big-roofed single-storey front, but less appropriate for the extended bulk added to the rear in 1910 by Peter Caldwell — it sits just off Main Street, empty and idle on a painted ocean of black tarmac, waiting sadly for the breakers.

Main Street itself is still lively. A twisting gable-to-gable spine, the scale of its buildings has been varied by changing needs: mixed in with one- and two-storey houses from the early 19th century are later tenement flats. **Woodrow's Building** turns the corner sweetly; in the shouldered bases of its front wall chimney stacks it has a date, 1835, and masonic signs; it was once the Masonic Arms.

Freeland Church (1826) comprises the Auld Licht Burghers' box kirk with the later addition of a hall (1857) in front, its gable surmounted by a pedimented temple bellcote. In 1912-13 Ramsay Traquair created a small chancel, removed a side gallery and added a new stair with lion's head skewputt outside and fanned timber roof inside. The **Post Office** has a crow-stepped gable centrepiece with fine timber dormers front and back.

From Lintwhite to Burngil, Main Street is unpretentious whatever the scale. Far more disruptive than changing heights or a few stylistic aberrations are the gaps and set-backs which interrupt the continuity of the street line. **Livery Walk** (1970), is calculated as a generous breathing space and, enhanced by Charles Anderson's mural, more or less acceptable. Beyond Torr Road the street disintegrates. Here and there, some 1820s' houses remain but all sense of enclosure has gone. Gone, too, by now is the railway, swinging away across the **Gryffe Viaduct** built with *corkscrew construction in the arches* by John King of Houston in 1868-69.

Gryffe Castle

Charles Wilson (1841)

Too grandly named, this much altered early work by Wilson is an asymmetrical mansion, with plain Classical detail and a square-columned porch no doubt culled from apprentice days with David Hamilton.

STRATHGRYFFE

South of the river the old road to Kilmacolm runs a leisurely course. Leaving Bridge of Weir at Torr
L Road, it reaches **Torr Hall** (1903-05), by James Souttar, an astonishing pile of grey Aberdeenshire granite commissioned by the wealthy Cargill family. A tall cylindrical tower soars above the main entrance to a machicolated and castellated viewing platform some 70 feet above ground; to its left, a heavily crow-stepped gable; to the right a two-storey block with four pedimented dormers.

M **Craigbet**

(18th century)

All is symmetry and restraint. The small, pavilion-roofed laird's house is thoroughly domestic in scale yet the axial approach across an open forecourt to the little porch on the eastern facade aspires clearly if parochially to a graceful Georgian lifestyle. The walls are roughcast but rustic quoining and another miniaturised porch leading to the walled garden on the west underline the claim to a distinction of modest means. Even the later single-storey wings north and south are suitably unassuming.

Walker

Walker

N **Carruth**

(from 1722)

Rebuilt 1782 and later extended during the 19th century, it has now been reduced and remodelled in an imaginative way by Macpherson & Bell. The south porch disappoints, but the north front, with its daringly corbelled room at eaves height, and calculated casualness in its fenestration, justifies the creative restoration adopted.

Top Craigbet.
Above Carruth, north front.

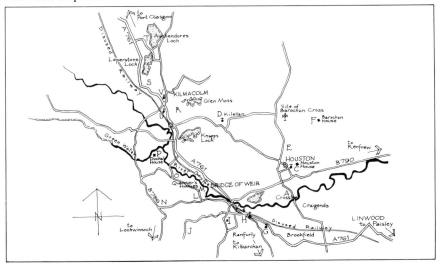

Duchal *was built by the Porterfield family who, in succession to the Lyles, had been lairds there since 1544. The Lyle home,* **Duchal Castle,** *of which almost nothing remains, had stood about a mile to the west on a steep outcrop of rock in a precipitous ravine between the Gryffe and a tributary stream — a near-island site which provided the family name de l'Isle, later Lyle. The Lyles proved powerful not only locally but nationally too. Too powerful at times! In 1488, after helping the young James IV to win the crown at the battle of Sauchieburn, Robert, Lord Lyle, was made Lord High Justiciar of Scotland.*

"But this honour did not satisfy his ambition. He and some of the other nobles deemed that their services had not been sufficiently acknowledged. The leader of the discontented faction was Lord Lennox who, with the co-operation of Lord Lyle and some others, organised an insurrection against the government, which broke out in 1489 . . . It did not prove a very serious affair, though the King thought it of sufficient importance to warrant him in marching against the rebels in person. He first besieged and took Lennox's Castle of Crookston, in the neighbourhood of Paisley, and from thence marched on Duchal."

The King's forces dragged heavy ordnance with them, including the great cannon, Mons Meg, still to be seen at Edinburgh Castle, but it seems more probable that Lyle surrendered than that any bombardment occurred. A few years later, indeed, James was back at Duchal on good terms with his host — and a certain Marion Boyd, kinswoman of the Lyles and one of several royal mistresses.

O **Quarrier's Homes**
Robert A. Bryden (from 1877)
Virtually a village in its own right. William Quarrier's amazing settlement for orphans grew and grew — Mount Zion Church (1888), sabbath school, residential homes, sanatoria, workshops, bakehouse, even a fire station. It is difficult not to feel that the responsibility weighed too heavily on Bryden. Everything is so squat: dumpy Tudor, broad swollen Baronial, coarsely massed Gothic; even the top-heavy church tower scarcely seems able to find release.

P **Duchal**
(1768)
In Renfrewshire terms, *a home of considerable magnitude* — three-storeys, five windows wide, with projecting pedimented centre bays front and rear each with Palladian motif doorpieces, the former on the *piano nobile* and reached by a spreading flying stair. In 1912 an earlier two-storey house (1710) which lay at the mansion's south-west corner was raised a further storey by John A. Campbell and A. D. Hislop. Though in a subservient scale, the result rather ruffles Duchal's dignity. To the west are formal gardens while on the other side of the house just south of a long avenue of trees running down to the Gryffe stands **Duchal Dovecote**, not unlike a diminutive Irish round tower.

Beyond Duchal Woods, the thick-set castellated tower of **Balrossie School** (1899) looks across the valley towards Kilmacolm. Once the Sailors' Orphans' Homes, by some corollary of institutional design perhaps its architects Hugh and David Barclay have given it that same strangely turbid quality found at Quarrier's.

Duchal House.

KILMACOLM

Two houses, standing sentinel at the eastern approach
to the village, set the tone. **Puldohran** (1913), a vast
red-tiled roof with twin-gabled white roughcast facade
by James Austen Laird is altogether English. Across
the road is **Wimborne** (1906) by the same architect: a
grey sandstone pile topped off with pedimented
dormers in turreted cones of grey-green slate; scarcely
rugged enough to be Baronial, but Scottish
nonetheless. Whereas rural nobility and gentry had
earlier espoused Baronial symbolism, the *nouveaux
riches* who came with the railway seemed seduced on
all fronts by English forms and the anglicised
aspirations of lawyer or banker, shipper or
shipbuilder, are everywhere evident in the
predominance of casements, half-timbering and red
tiles. The permutations are endless — though rarely as
restrained as the Cotswold-like **Knapps** (1913), by T.
Andrew Millar, on Houston Road. Of course, crow-
steps, roughcast and slate are present, too, but, more
often than not a softer English style of building lines
the leafy roads of this lovely village.

The counter claims of English and Scots precedent
are particularly clear in the series of villas which
James Salmon built in Kilmacolm between 1898 and
1908. **Rowantreehill** (1898), Rowantreehill Road,
where the Salmons lived, soars on its hilltop site; like
the flanks of a medieval Scottish keep, solid dominates
over void. Yet above this high gaunt base has been
perched all the striped and dormered fussiness of
Tudor. English on Scottish it may be, but there is no
victory here for the South, for Salmon achieves
precisely that combination of *sheer walls and the most
unexpected crustaceous projections on top* which
characterises the Scottish Castle. Nor is this all;

Kilmacolm from the east.

Rowantreehill.

Walker

strange *gargoyle* figures, oddly profiled rafter ends, and some fluid stone carving around the entrance, impart an *Art Nouveau* mystery to the whole romantic conceit. Later additions by James Miller in 1914 barely impair Salmon's success.

Bishop's House (1904), formerly Miyanoshita, on Porterfield Road, is stiff, severe and a little forbidding. **Hazelhope** (1906), downhill on Gryffe Road, has a fidgety but cosy English intimacy. **Den o'Gryffe**, by the riverside beyond Knockbuckle Road, began in 1905 in similar cottage vein; but eighteen months later Salmon extended his design with a startling children's wing cleverly fused to the earlier house. Despite half-timbering in the connection of new to old, the nursery block is fresh and uncompromising — a white octagonal box, the roof gathered pyramidally around a stumpy central stack; there is more than a hint of the 30s in its clean geometry and horizontal window panes. Den o'Gryffe's neighbour, **Nether Knockbuckle** (1907), maintains this evolution; a two-storey white box with chamfered corners, this time oversailed by a high tiled roof. English allusions linger, but the powerful clarity of form, especially plastic in the swollen chimney stacks which buttress each end gable, produces a palpably solid Scottishness.

Top Den o'Gryffe.
Above Nether Knockbuckle.
Right Windyhill; east and west elevations drawn by C. R. Mackintosh.

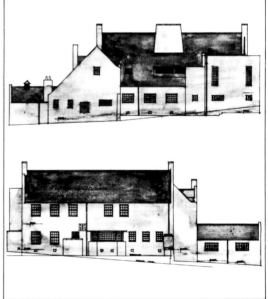

Hunterian Museum

Windyhill
C. R. Mackintosh (1899-1901)
This is the first of Mackintosh's *Houses on Hills*, and, like Hill House at Helensburgh which followed, it is an austere black and white affair. The west elevation

RCAHMS

looking down across a tumbling romantic garden over Strathgryffe, could be mistaken for a farmhouse — were it not for the flat-roofed bay of the living room and a tell-tale hint of preciousness in the arrangement of windows. To the east, the elements have much less composure, and are all the better for that. The technique is honest aggregation, seen in deliberate exposure across the dipping cope of the garden wall.

There is more Mackintosh to be seen in Kilmacolm. In the cemetery, the **Reid Gravestone** (1898), a Spook School sepulchre; on the main Port Glasgow Road **Auchenbothie Lodge** (1901), a slated pyramid on a square plan with gratuitous buttress; at **Auchenbothie Mains** two humble alteration jobs, one of which has an unusual splay-plan gable originally crow-stepped.

S **Auchenbothie House**
William Leiper (1898)
A picturesquely grouped composition (1898) in cosy Baronial, made softer and warmer by its materials — roughcast with red sandstone dressings and features.

T **Cloak**
C. R. Mackintosh (from 1906)
Begun by Mackintosh as a *ploughman's cottage*, altered and extended by him in 1908 and again in 1912-13, and by others later, this complex house, set beside Auchendores Reservoir, has grown gauchely. Perhaps it is as well that such a conglomerate has been drowned in ivy.

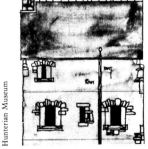

Hunterian Museum

Top Auchenbothie House.
Middle and bottom Cloak; east and north elevations of original ploughman's cottage drawn by C. R. Mackintosh.

Kilmacolm Cross and the Old Kirk.

Kilmacolm is more than an up-market ghetto of large houses. Origins as a rural and religious settlement give it a coherent core with a crossroads centre lying in a dipping double bend on the road to Port Glasgow. Here there is a change in scale and a strange tension exerted between the towers of the two village churches.

St Columba Church.

U **St Columba Church**
William Leiper (1901-03)
Formerly St James, Leiper's last church is in finely cut Decorated Revival. The tower, finished in a crocketted saddle-back roof with corner turret, has been called *Franco-Scotto*, but the aisled nave leading to a raised chancel has little to do with the tradition of the reformed Scottish kirk.

V **The Old Kirk**
James Dempster (1831)
To the north, where a church has stood since the 13th century — a typically plain box church, balconied, with tall two-light lancets and a castellated belfry tower. In 1890 John Honeyman reconstituted the remnants of a 13th century chancel as a vestry, now the **Murray Chapel**. Medieval lancets and a piscina can be seen. In 1902-03 the roof was removd and a new open-beamed ceiling created, a galleried transept added and a new pulpit, table, font and organ installed. At the time, the **Porterfield Tomb** (1560) was repositioned as an awkwardly composite monument in the graveyard wall of the new transept.

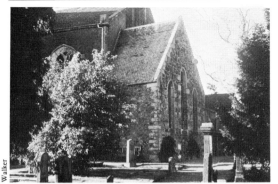

Walker

The Rev. James Murray *in his parish history of Kilmacolm (1907) tells of a discovery made at the time of the 1902-03 alterations to the Old Kirk. Demolishing the old pulpit workmen found a manuscript concealed in the hollow of the supporting pillar. Placed there unofficially it recorded the names of some of the tradesmen involved in building the 1831 church and concluded: "At this moment the people and aristocracy are contesting their rights and priviledges (sic). May the people triumph and may you transmit unsullied to your children the Glorius (sic) Freedom which we of to-day are so determined to transmit unsullied to you." As Murray writes, "One can recognise the sentiments, that were doubtless very widespread just on the eve of the passing of the Reform Bill".*

Burnside Place and **Rachel Place** (early 19th century) give some sense of an older, lower streetscape. But **Lyle Buildings, Octavia Buildings** and **Norval Place** (1873), sharing a varied eaves line of chimneyed pediments and dormers, are tenements in scale and plan. So, too, are **St James Terrace** (1903), by Burnet, Boston & Carruthers, and the crow-stepped twin-gabled **Market Place**. Past the Old Kirk up High Street is **Overton Terrace** (1903), James Austen Laird again; a splendid red sandstone block with *Art Nouveau* tiles in the closes. Some distance on up Finlaystone Road, **Water Yetts** (1772) can be found surrounded by not the worst local authority housing.

There is much new residential building in Kilmacolm — too much indeed — and most little able to hold its own alongside the quality of the past. Ronald Sheridan has created a pleasant group of houses at **Willow Drive** (1973), varied in form but unified by material. On Duchal Road, **Atrium** (1980), Burnet, Bell and Partners, attains real sophistication — even if its superb detailing scarcely succeeds in compensating for the intrusion of a flat roof among the villas of Duchal Road.

Above Murray Chapel, Old Kirk.
Below Atrium, Duchal Road.

Burnet, Bell

SOUTH BANK OF THE CLYDE

As might be expected, close links between Renfrew and Glasgow have existed over a long period. In 1136 the Church at Renfrew was one of King David I's gifts to the newly consecrated Glasgow Cathedral. Thereafter no doubt the clergy at Glasgow ministered to Renfrew; certainly Gerard of Rome, whose name survives from the middle of the 13th century, was both canon of Glasgow and priest in Renfrew. Some two hundred years later, at the foundation of Glasgow University, Renfrew's priest, Duncan Bunch, became a regent and later Rector at the University. Andrew Hay, first Protestant minister of Renfrew, was also Rector; prominent not only in the religious and educational affairs of his day but deeply involved in politics too. He was implicated in the murder of Queen Mary's secretary David Riccio in 1556 and banished to Dunbar.

Strathclyde Region

Renfrew Town Hall.

RENFREW

When Thomas Pennant sailed down the Clyde past Renfrew in 1792 he found *the country town . . . an inconsiderable place*. Not much has changed. For all its ancient origins — a royal charter granted by Robert III in 1396, and royal burgh status dating back to the reign of David I — the town has never amounted to much economically. Certainly it could never match the wealth nor the architectural distinction of Greenock or Paisley.

In 1710, Crawfurd in his *General Description of the Shire of Renfrew* recorded only *one principal street,*

about half a mile in length, with some small lanes . . . a spacious Market-place and a handsome Town-house.
Over a century later, in 1818, Robertson could add little — although he was able to refer to Elderslie House, a building *of palatial proportions* and to the new mansion of Campbell of Blythswood. William Cobbett's visit to Renfrew was highlighted by his dining *with Mr Speirs at his beautiful seat near the Clyde at Elderslie where I saw some as beautiful trees as I ever saw in the whole course of my life.* **Elderslie House** (1776-82) and its estate were, however, destroyed in 1924 to be replaced later by the mini Battersea of Braehead Power Station (1946-51). Downriver on the north-western side of the town, Gillespie Graham's Greek Revival **Blythswood House** (1820-22), its architectural severity all the more potent for lavish planting, has also disappeared (demolished 1935) beneath the fairways of a golf course. Besides its trees, all that remains from the great days of the Ranfield or Blythswood Estate are the iron arrow-headed riverside railings built no doubt to deter those Highland drovers who, as Sir Walter Scott on a visit to his kinsman Col. Campbell of Blythswood in 1827 wrote in his diary, *break down his fences in order to pay a visit to the place,* and thus avoid the toll charges they would otherwise have been forced to pay for using the roads.

Blythswood House (demolished 1935).

A **Town Hall**
James Lamb (1871-73)
Renfrew still has *a handsome Town house.* Not the Tolbooth (c. 1670) that MacGibbon and Ross chose to record despite its having been *taken down some years ago,* but a latter-day Town Hall erected on the same site at the The Cross in a *mixed French-Gothic* design by Paisley architect James Lamb. In 1877, fire destroyed much of the new structure and rebuilding was necessary. The work, supervised by Loudon McQueen, clerk of works on the Blythswood Estate, restored the Gothic hall and offices, created a balustraded flat roof and raised a taller turretted tower to dominate the centre of town.

> *Externally the building presents much the same appearance as hitherto, with the exception of the tower. It has been made more sky-piercing, or, possibly, as one of the Councillors remarked at a late meeting, 'gingerbread-like'.*

Today this tower stands at the end of a widened High Street which runs south-eastwards towards Glasgow. On the right, at **6-24 High Street** (1926-26) are shops and flats built by the Renfrew Equitable Co-operative Society Ltd., stretching to the kirkyard.

Renfrew District

Above Old Parish Church.
Below Bank of Scotland and 5-17 High Street.
Bottom Masonic Temple.

Carson & Hunter

B **Old Parish Church**
J. T. Rochead (1861-62)
The style is lancet Gothic, yet broad-based and squat rather than elongated, although the elegantly simple broach spire, *one of the most beautiful in the country*, manages to soar free. The plan, obliquely set to the surrounding street pattern, is cruciform and incorporates later alterations to the chancel (1908) by P. MacGregor Chalmers. Within the church are two late medieval sepulchral monuments: the **Ross Vault** (1633), an arched recess with the customary recumbent effigies of husband and wife; and the plainer **Motherwell Monument,** an altar tomb which may date from the 15th century.

Marking the corner with Canal Street is the dunce's cap turret of the **Bank of Scotland** by George Washington Browne; four storeys of red sandstone ashlar with decorative detail in a free classical vein (dolphin capitals in the arched windows!). From **5 to 17 High Street** (1981-83) Scott, Brownrigg and Turner match the scale and colour of the Co-op buildings with some trim red brick housing — shops again on the ground floor, but a mansarded second floor attic. A walk down Queen

C Street reveals Daniel McMath's **Masonic Temple** (1931); precisely named, its precise facade is, in fact, a mini Doric temple, set symmetrically at first floor on a wider lower storey. Farther east, a few isolated tenements, some very ordinary council housing and then the long tree-lined boulevard route through industrial no-man's-land to Glasgow.

North of The Cross there is a denser more urban feel to the streets. From **10-48 Canal Street** (1900-01) four-storeyed red sandstone tenements give

Carson & Hunter

In June 1838 *Archibald Campbell, Lord Blythswood, died. Three weeks later a group of "Noblemen and Gentlemen of the County" met in Paisley to set up a subscription fund for some form of Blythswood Testimonial. An infirmary, a church and a "house of refuge" were among suggestions made in preference to any monument or "unmeaning stack-like column", but in the end it was decided to build a school. An architectural competition was held and, from twenty two entries, that of Scott, Stephen and Gale was chosen. John Stephen's design is still full of inventive decorum: a sacrophagus sits atop the pediment, draped urns flank the portico, the Tower of the Winds and the Lysicrates Monument are combined in a single balanced steeple composition. A noble but delicate gravitas.*

Brown Institute.

scale and some distinction, notably at **48** where a pudding basin dome ends the street wall with assurance. Left over from an earlier street-scape, the **Wheatsheaf Inn** (c. 1830) might be unremarkable were it not for the vegetal relief ornament *hanging* between architraved windows and a 1666 datestone. At 41 Canal Street the square-snecked red rubble front of the **Brown Institute** (1903) pushes out a wide battlemented bay over its compressed central entrance. **Renfield Street** has more high red tenements in the midst of which **Renfrew North Church** (rebuilt 1882) intrudes uneasily. At the end of Renfield Street's tenements space funnels out generously around John Stephen's **Blythswood Testimonial School** (1840-42) one of the loveliest but most disregarded monuments of the Greek Revival in Scotland.

Beyond this built-up area around The Cross, the closer one comes to the Clyde the bleaker the prospect. Another red tenement, stranded at **11 Meadowside Street** (c. 1910), has an Edwardian pub front and *Art Nouveau* tiles in the close. At the river bank the **Ferry Inn** (1829), 1 Clyde Street, an L-plan gabled house with Roman Doric pilastered doorpiece and wide eaves cornice, is a quiet spot now — no longer a stop-off for scores of thirsty workers on their way home from the yards. A ferry still runs, but not the thronged chain ferry that for a hundred years or so — before the construction of the Clyde Tunnel and the Erskine Bridge — linked Renfrew with Yoker.

Blythswood Testimonial School.

Top 1 Hairst Street.
Above Porterfield Road.

Victory Baths.

Most of Renfrew's growth has taken place south of the Cross. Gambling with Baroque, T. G. Abercrombie's **1 Hairst Street** (c. 1910), formerly the Union Bank and now a betting shop, has a symmetrical concave-convex front with hemicycle porch. **Trinity Church** (1864-65), Paisley Road, is a small cruciform kirk built in a rudimentary Gothic enlivened by an octagonal pinnacle belfry. There are pleasant cottage villas at **39 Paisley Road** and **29** and **31 Glebe Street,** but the bulk — and the best — of the building on this side of town has resulted from successive waves of inter-war municipal housing.

In 1919, *Homes for Heroes* cottage housing was begun at **Victory Gardens** but later schemes attempted denser more urban solutions. Many of these were remarkably inventive; Hamilton Neil's housing south of Newmains Road, around **Tinto Square,** successfully combines a variety of national motifs — conical turrets, dormers, etc. — with the corner windows and parapetted planar surfaces of Thirties' international Modernism. Paisley architect James Steel Maitland continued this idiosyncratic confection of old and new, in his **Porterfield Road** schemes (1935-39) and at **Cocklesloan** (1940s). By the time he published his views on *Scottish Housing Past and Present* in the *RIBA Journal* in 1952 he had built more than one thousand houses in Renfrew alone.

Not far south of The Cross, where the long straight tenement terrace of Paisley Road begins, the A8, runs west to follow the south bank of the slowly widening Clyde estuary at Inchinnan Road. To the right are the **Victory Baths** (1921) by T. G. Abercrombie, an ashlar front with pedimented eaves dormers and a central circular stair tower ogee-domed.

Renfrew District

In April 1685 *Argyle returned from exile in Holland with about 300 men, landing first at Campbeltown where he increased his invading force to over 2,000. Indecision over strategy, however, frustrated success, the King's army stemmed the rebels' advance and, though Argyle himself chose to attempt an attack on Glasgow, treachery stranded him at Old Kilpatrick. He forded the Clyde making for Renfrew but was easily captured. After a night as a prisoner in the Place of Paisley (q.v.), he was taken to Edinburgh and, on the last day of June 1685, beheaded at the Mercat Cross. Two shapeless unlettered stones are his pathetic memorial.*

The Argyle Stone.

Alongside, still more Scottish, is A. N. Paterson's **Police Station** (1910), its broad square keep, parapetted and asymmetrically-turretted, rising sternly above Abercrombie's more humane nationalism. Opposite the junction with Bell Street is Cowan and Watson's neat black and white **St James's Church** (1093), a shed nave with aisles, simple pointed windows and a rather perfunctorily Gothic air.

Inchinnan Road crosses the old railway line from Paisley and passes Kirklandneuk to the south — housing by J. Steel Maitland from the early 1950s; **Community Centre** (1980) in vernacular modern by David Rae — to reach the White Cart. To the north, the fringes of Blythswood Estate have managed to absorb the industrial architecture of suburban shopping, a large hotel and the cars that go with both, without sacrificing too much of the wooded landscape that Pennant, sailing downriver, described as *the most elegant and softest of any in North Britain*. Hidden in these trees, near the east bank of the Cart, is the **Argyle Stone** — two stone relics, in fact, protected by iron railings but weathered beyond signification. Said to come from an ancient cross that marked the shrine of St Conval, whose activities in the neighbourhood had given rise to a kind of Dark Ages Lourdes, the monument has, by some oecumenical freak of fate, become associated with the Protestant rebellion of the 17th century Earl of Argyle.

Police Station.

Renfrew District

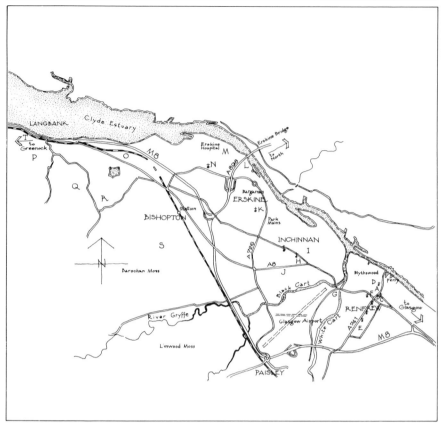

INCHINNAN

In 1772 a new road was completed between Glasgow and Greenock. Beyond Renfrew, at the *Spout of Renfrewshire*, it crossed the confluence of the White and Black Cart rivers passing over a wooden swing bridge, built in 1787 across the navigable canal east of the White Cart, and then over *the most important bridge in Renfrewshire*, a nine-arched stone span constructed in 1759. In 1809, however, flooding destroyed this crossing and two new **Inchinnan Bridges** (1809-12), each of three wide segmental spans with niched and columned piers, had to be built. Designed by engineer Robertson Buchanan, the bridges still serve: with the steel bascule bridge of 1923 on the edge of Blythswood Estate they carry the A8 traffic west towards Greenock.

Across the rivers is the **Campbell Mausoleum** (1838), a flat-topped earthen mound in which are interred the ashes of the laird of Blythswood, Archibald Campbell. Close by is the ancient site of St Conval's Kirk of Inchinnan, once the church of the Knights Templars.

"Ane halie man of Scotland of great fame
That samin tyme hecht Conwallus by name
Discipill als he wes of Saint Nungow
In Inch annane schort gait bewist Glasgow
His bodie lys quair I myself hes been
In pilgrimage and his reliques hes seen."

RCAHMS

Inchinnan Parish Church
(demolished).

Both tomb and kirk were flight path victims in the
development of Glasgow Airport: the former, isolated
and neglected under runway lights; the latter, i.e.
Rowand Anderson's Church of All Hallows of 1903,
totally razed. At **Inchinnan Parish Church**
(1965-66), however, Miller and Black's replacement
kirk incorporates several of Anderson's Decorated
windows in an assemblage of flat-roofed roughcast
boxes. Other gestures to Inchinnan's sacred past are
equally sad: several medieval lithic fragments removed
from the old site have been arranged in a dull pebble
garden, while three Celtic stones lie in the carport
porch beneath a self-consciously *modern* campanile,
triangular in plan and obliquely sliced off in section
above its open belfry.

Inchinnan Bridges illustrated in
Wilson's *General View of the
Agriculture of Renfrewshire,* 1812.

101

Northbar House.

Renfrew District

Inchinnan village retains a few vestiges of charm.
Greenhead (c. 1800) is a skew-gabled farmhouse
rubble-built with minimally dressed margins, flanked
by lower piended wings which return around an overgrown courtyard to the south. There are a few old
cottages and, at Broomlands, on the corner of
Luckinsford Road, **Park Church** (1849), formerly the
Free Church, a dumpy lancetted T-plan kirk with a
low stone spire. North of the old road, out of sight in
the wood behind **Beardmore Cottages** (1919), is
Northbar House (c. 1742) crow-stepped, three
storeys and severely plain but for the armorial panel of
the Gilchrist family who built it.

On the open road to the south is the once
stunningly white palace of the **India Tyre Factory**
(1929-30) by Wallis, Gilbert and Partners, a long Art
Deco treat of giant order splayed pilasters framing two
storeys of metal windows, originally chevron glazed.
Fluted mouldings delineate the parapet and sills, and
green, red and black tiles enliven capitals, plinth and
entrance portal. Amazingly, the building has been
abandoned — ironically inexplicable, since, less than
half a mile west, are the fresh factories of a greenfield
industrial estate.

At the Red Smiddy the A726 crosses the Greenock
Road. Past **Newmains,** a polychromatic brick villa-
farm, a road runs on over flat country crossing the
Black Cart at **Barnsford Bridge** (1793, rebuilt 1909,
demolished 1985) until, skirting Glasgow Airport (*q.v.*)
it reaches Paisley. All trace of the triangularly planned
Walkinshaw (1791, demolished 1927), *certainly the
most extraordinary of all the houses* by Robert Adam,
has gone.

Below India of Inchinnan Tyre
Factory.
Bottom Walkinshaw (demolished).

RIAS

Paisley Museum

Miller

ERSKINE

Bargarran Centre.

Like every other post-war new town, Erskine is a disorientating network of roads. Signposts proclaim a *Town Centre* but this is, as yet, elusive. Shops at **Bargarran Centre** (1972), by T. M. Miller and Partners, a cluster of copper-clad monopitches, provide only a minimal sense of community focus. But there are schools, a supermarket, a pub and some new
K churches. At Rashielee, **New Erskine Parish Church** (1977), by George B. Horspool, is a busy agglomeration of roughcast walls, some with deep lead-lined parapets, behind which a curved monopitch rises to a belfry peak. Less picturesquely sited on Barwood Road, the **Church of St John Bosco** (1978), by Wagner Associates, is simpler and tidier, its jutting slated room alternatively yacht prow or jib sail according to view.

It is housing at Erskine that merits most commendation. Although there is now a growing blight of routine spec-built suburbia eating up the countryside, much of the earlier development is of high quality, cleverly grouped, varied in skyline, and often supremely well landscaped.

Two buildings rise above the pervasive domestic scale: the **Crest Hotel** (1970-71) by Morris and Steedman — six bedroom floors of ribbed concrete eggcrate on a two-storeyed brick plinth — and the
L long brown brick offices of the AA's **Fanum House** (1974) by Sir Basil Spence, Glover and Ferguson, which complements its more modest height with a sleek sophistication of detail.

Below New Erskine Parish Church.
Bottom Fanum House seen below Erskine Bridge.

Spence, Glover, Ferguson

Horspool

RCAHMS

Erskine House illustrated in Millar's *Castles & Mansions of Renfrewshire*, 1889.

Elsewhere in the 360 acres of the Erskine policies are the remnants of former days: lodge houses, estate workers' cottages, and "on a conspicuous situation . . . an elegant column", the 80' BLANTYRE OBELISK (1831) raised in memory of the 11th Lord Blantyre, accidentally shot in the 1830 Revolution in Brussels! The design is by Smirke's pupil William Burn.

Old Erskine Parish Church.

Renfrew District

M **Erskine House**
Sir Robert Smirke (1828)
Across Old Ferry Road — now a *cul-de-sac* since the building of **Erskine Bridge** (1967-71) made the old chain ferry redundant — lies the demesne of Erskine Estate. In 1703 this pleasant sweep of land was bought by the 5th Baron Blantyre, and in 1828 the 11th Lord commissioned Smirke, architect of the British Museum, to build a new mansion house on gently sloping ground just south of the Clyde. No exercise in metropolitan Grecian gravity but a vast Elizabethan Revival pile, its balustraded eaves is interrupted by frequent pinnacles and curvilinear gables. The plan, symmetrical except for a high Gothic *porte-cochère* and low service wing, is arranged along the east-west spine of the Long Gallery, largest of several immensely tall apartments. The interiors — *Georgian Gothic* — are magnificent. Since 1916 these flat-vaulted halls have served, surely with lofty intimidation, as The Princess Louise Scottish Hospital for Limbless Sailors and Soldiers. But fortunately not only these for whatever else may be thought about the grand-manner planning of the flat-roofed convalescent blocks (1950-63) tied into the north-south axis of the main house, they are at least in more human scale. So, too, are some fifty cottages variously built in the extensive grounds since the last war. But most endearing of all are the original Stables, Kennels, and Piggery *all very substantial buildings, and in some respects works of art* — especially the octagonal Gothic **Piggery,** now alas in ruins.

N **Old Erskine Parish Church**
David Hamilton (1813-14)
The simple ashlar church, bearing the Blantyre motto *Sola juvat virtus* (Virtue alone delights), is a galleried Gothic Revival nave having a battlemented tower to the west and a low octagonal vestry, also battlemented, brilliantly added at the south-east by W. D. McLennan in 1902-03.

BISHOPTON

Although the village has swollen into a characterless dormitory suburb, strung out along the road a few rubble cottages, from early 19th century or before, still stand between **8 Greenock Road** and the **Golf Inn. Rossland Church** (1843), a primitive hall kirk with a broad gable belfry, survives too despite its sagging roof. Variegated and brash, the **Community Library** (1984), by Renfrew District Council architects, brightens the scene.

Beyond the village the road breasts the hill to reveal the estuary of the Clyde. From Bishopton, to Wemyss Bay the prospect rarely disappears. At the Convent of the Good Shepherd the sisters enjoy it from **Bishopton House,** first of several Scottish mansions in the area. Recast (1916-20) in a severe stone idiom by Paisley architect J. Craig Barr, it incorporates vaulted cellars and other remnants from a 17th century house in a romantic composition overlooking the river.

RCAHMS

Renfrew District

Top Bishopton House.
Above Gleddoch House.
Below Clyde Estuary west from above Bishopton.

Gleddoch House
A. N. Paterson (1926-27)
Again nationalist in form, though this time Scots Renaissance: it presents a symmetrical front to the river flanked by ogee roofed square towers. Now a hotel, a new bedroom wing (1979) by Mansfield Design Partnership has been well integrated to the south. **Gleddoch Country Club** (1975), a little uphill, maintains slate and roughcast too, but with rather less care.

Drums is more Baronial. From 1898-1900 the existing house of 1770 was re-worked for the shipbuilding Lithgows with all the picturesque accretions of the style to such an extent that its Georgian symmetries were totally obscured. At the same time a separate stables block, equally in thrall to the delights of calculated disorder, was added.

Beyond Bishopton the road breasts the hill to reveal the estuary of the Clyde. It is a spectacular view; one which John Galt, leaving Greenock as a young man in 1804, gazed on with saddened affection. "On the morning when I bade adieu to Greenock, my father accompanied me in the post-chaise which was to convey me early enough to meet the London mailcoach at Glasgow. The air was bright and calm, but I was exceedingly depressed. During the first stage scarcely a word was exchanged, and while the horses were changed at the Bishopton Inn, the usual stage in those days between Greenock and Glasgow, I walked back on the fields above with no buoyant heart.

The view towards Argyleshire from the brow of the hill, is perhaps one of the most picturesque in the world. I have since seen some of the finest scenes, but none superior. At the time it seemed as if some pensive influence rested on the mountains, and silently allured me back. . . ."

Walker

Formakin, drawn by Robert
Lorimer, 1908.

R **Formakin**
Robert Lorimer (from 1903)
About a mile to the south along the B789 this is a
masterpiece of crafted deceit. When the Paisley
stockbroker J. A. Holms came here in 1903 only an
old meal mill and a few farm dwellings existed.
Within a decade Holms and his architect had transformed the scene. They began with the landscaping of
the estate and the layout of new formal gardens, built
gate lodges and stables (1907), continued with garages,
pig-sties and *bothy* tower house (1909), and all but
completed a large mansion house (1910-11) to house
Holms's collection of tapestries, carpets, and other
valuable art objects. Everything was conceived in *the
purest Scotch I've ever done*, as Lorimer put it, and
constructed, whether in stone, brick, timber or
reinforced concrete, to the highest standards of
craftsmanship. Formakin has its humorous side —
mischievous stone monkeys clamber over ridges and a
carved datestone (*1694*) above the entrance to the
stables courtyard is accompanied by the letters DL —
Damned Lie! But the great house is an eerie place, too,
for unfinished and unoccupied, it has stood waiting a
lifetime for life since Holms ran out of money just
before World War I. Rescued by Renfrew District
Council as part of a Country Park, its future looks
assured.

S **Dargavel House**
(from 16th century)
Frozen in the limbo of forbidden territory behind the
fences of the Royal Ordnance Factory, it can barely be
seen — a Z-plan house of late 16th or 17th century
provenance with Baronial additions (1849) by David
Bryce and further alterations (1910) by Peter
Macgregor Chalmers.

RCAHMS

LANGBANK

Back by the Clyde, the road from Bishopton dips down to Langbank, stretched out, as its name suggests, along the estuary shore. A string of villas, some with unusually decorative bargeboards, ends at **Woodside Cottages** (1850-52), a *cottage orné* terrace built in a mix of red sandstone and whin, tentatively identified as an early work of Alexander *Greek* Thomson. Otherwise, only the thrice-fallen, thrice-rebuilt, spire of **Langbank Parish Church** (1866-67), formerly the U.F. Church, catches the eye.

T **Finlaystone House**
(from c. 1760)

Past the village is Finlaystone Estate, patrimony of the Cunninghams of Glencairn. The house was, in Burns' day, a *fyne house, well planted, with good inclosures and gardens*, largely the work of John Douglas. Now, the Georgian mansion is buried beneath the rather heavy-handed remodelling J. J. Burnet effected between 1898 and 1903. For all that, Burnet's loggia to the forecourt on the east and his massively columned staircase hall lend Finlaystone a robust grandeur.

Finlaystone Estate *is the patrimony of the Cunninghams of Glencairn. Here, in 1556, the 5th Earl entertained the Reformer John Knox who "ministrat the Lordis Table" during his stay. Almost 250 years later, another guest, Robert Burns — doubtless a more convivial one — scratched his initials on a window pane in the library; they can still be seen, perhaps an appropriate memento to Scottish letters and to the affection Burns held for his patron, James Cunningham, the 14th Earl of Glencairn. On Cunningham's death in 1791, Burns wrote a Lament. It is not his most memorable poetry, however, and his prose makes better reading. "My heart glows, and shall ever glow, with the most grateful sense and remembrance of his lordship's goodness. . . . Nor shall my gratitude perish with me. If among my children I shall have a son that has a heart, he shall hand it down to his child as a family honour, and a family debt, that my dearest existence I owe to the noble house of Glencairn."*

Left Finlaystone House.
Below Dargavel House.

RCAHMS

Port Glasgow in 1825, seen from the east.

Inverclyde District Libraries

Below Broadfield Hospital, formerly Broadstone House, from the west.
Bottom Clune Park Church.

RCAHMS

Walker

PORT GLASGOW

The approach to Port Glasgow from the east is splendidly scenic. Nor is the view suddenly revealed on the high road from Kilmacolm any less spectacular — a magnificent panorama stretching across the Firth from spikey shipyard cranes in the foreground to the distant rounded backs of the Cowal hills.

Broadfield Hospital
David Bryce (1869-70)
Sitting high above the shore road, a Scots-Baronial mansion in greyish pink square-snecked sandstone. There is a high entrance tower, turretted on the north-west, some finely carved and inscribed eaves dormers, and a rather special stone-framed conservatory part of which, octagonal on plan, has a glazed dome and cupola — *one of the finest of such buildings anywhere in Britain.* All of this more than holds its own in the natural scene. Further along the wooded hillside to the west, however, **Langlands Park** (1888-89), though more boldly sited, is less architecturally assertive.

Development through Woodhall and Clune Park is dominated by successive series of relentlessly ordinary tenements. Nothing here to merit attention. Except perhaps **Clune Park School** (1887), by Hugh and David Barclay, a high two-storey building with an 8-bay pilastrade at first floor and jubilee busts of Victoria and Albert. **Clune Park Church** (1905), by Boston, Menzies and Morton, has quite the most

St Mary's Episcopal Church.

lovely *Art Nouveau* Gothic traceried window filling the gable above a verandah-like porch.

No such architectural relief is to be found uphill in Bardrainney, Boglestone or Devol, where the natural landscape has all but vanished in tracts of inter-war and post-war housing — none except Frank Burnet, Bell and Partners' **St Mary's Episcopal Church** (1983-84) a trim if sometimes fussy replacement, in orange brick and copper roofing, for the original Newark church (1856-57) sacrificed to motorway convenience. Yet turn a corner in this cold built-up hillside and there is still escape in that recurring prospect out over the town below to the wide estuary. The river is always there. Looking down Clune Brae only the most brutalised spirit could fail to be lifted by the Firth shimmering in summer evening sunlight. And then, too, even the silhouetted tenement gables stepping back up **Bouverie Street** (c. 1870) become one of the town's great sights.

Bouverie Street tenements.

109

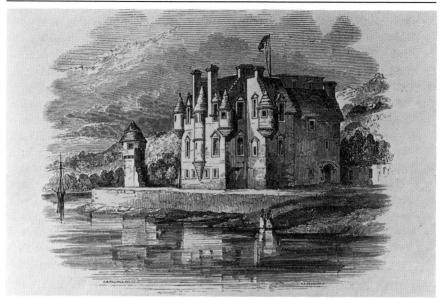

*When **Billings** wrote about Newark in the early 1850s he began by remarking how "The many thousands of summer travellers along the Firth of Clyde, whether by steamboat or railway, can scarcely forget a massive brown edifice, decayed but not ruined, rising with its square tower and rich cluster of cones and chimneys, in singular contrast to the spruce newness of Greenock, Port Glasgow and the villas of the Glasgow merchants studded here and there along the sloping banks of the majestic estuary." There is no steamer now and Port Glasgow is neither spruce nor new, but Newark is in excellent repair and its irregular skyline with the Saltire flying a memorable and surprising contrast to the surrounding scene.*

Newark Castle
(from 15th century)

At the foot of Clune Brae, despite its now incongruous setting, Newark is still *a fine specimen of our Scottish Domestic Architecture of an advanced type.* There are three parts to the building: a tall square keep (c. 1484) at the south-east; on the south-west a contemporary gatehouse through which a vaulted entrance passage leads into the original courtyard; and finally, linking the two earlier towers, the more extensive three-storey L-plan buildings (doorway dated 1597, dormer 1599) erected by Patrick Maxwell to provide *more modern* and prepossessing accommodation. The planning of this latest section of Newark is certainly advanced: there is a generous scale-and-platt stair in the north-east corner and an attempt has clearly been made to achieve symmetry along the riverside facade.

At **6-8 Newark Street** (1770) the old Post Office is a relic from the earliest streets. Uphill are the four-storey tenements of Bouverie Street. Downhill, industry has wrought a staggering change of scale with the former **Gourock Ropeworks** (c. 1885), a seven-storey building in polychromatic brick with blind porthole motifs at the highest level. Next to this are two dilapidated and derelict Georgian town houses — **102-104 Bay Street** (c. 1820) and **98-100** (c. 1820). Still in use is **90 Bay Street** (c. 1850) a tenement with corner windows that curve attractively to meet each end gable. Further on, the street line is lost in recent point-block development; not until Fore Street is a genuinely urban quality properly established.

Town Buildings

David Hamilton (1815)
Somewhat isolated and enfeebled now that the
calculated relationship of a sturdy Doric tetrastyle
portico and 150 foot high Classical steeple *(c.f.* Falkirk)
with the broad harbourside space of Fore Street has
been ruined, this is still the dominant architectural
monument in Port Glasgow, marking the town centre
with considerable dignity.

With the elimination of the wide waterfront, the
old harbours vanished and the graving dock (1762,
improved 1873-74) which lay behind the Town
Buildings was filled in after over two hundred years'
service. On the shore side of Fore Street, however,
part of the original grid-iron street layout has survived
sustaining the sense that this is the centre of town.

During the late 1660s the Town Council of
Glasgow authorised approaches to obtain land to build
a harbour for the city down river. Rejected by
Dumbarton and Troon and baulked by Greenock, in
1668 Glasgow acquired lands from Sir Patrick
Maxwell of Newark and, obtaining a Crown Charter
empowering them to build the *port and harbour of
Glasgow,* resolved upon the construction of the new
town of Newport. It was not until 1693, however, that
the city undertook to *draw ane draught of the haill
ground ther . . .* and a year later sent Francis
Stevenson to

> *measure the ground and divide it in plotts for building
> houses and chalking out of streets and lands, and to
> draw the ground plott thereof, that it may be a rule
> for the tyme to come . . .*

Confirmed in a plan drawn up by John Ainslie a
hundred years later, Stevenson's regularised layout
formed the basis for the 18th century development. By
then the town of Newport had coalesced with the
older village of Newark to form the burgh of Port
Glasgow.

This grid remains today — although the
redevelopment of the Bay Area (1909-12), designed by
George Arthur & Son, and largely financed by the
shipbuilding Lithgow family, swept away many of the
buildings of the old town to make way for red
sandstone tenements. The facades, of bay windows
and heavy rustication, are consistent and emphasise
the street corners with pudding basin domes trapped
between tall chimney stacks. **John Wood Street**
(1912) — most of its shopfronts and fascias intact, and
a fine golden fish projecting at **no. 13** — is best, its
four storeys stepping up the hill to the station where
it ends in the curving facade of the **Star Hotel** (1910).
King Street, three storeys, is plainer but includes at

Walker

Town Buildings.

Opposite top Newark Castle from
Billings's *The Ecclesiastical &
Baronial Antiquities of Scotland.*
Below Gourock Ropeworks.

Below John Wood Street.
Bottom Star Hotel.

Inverclyde District Libraries

Inverclyde District Libraries

In April 1812, the "Comet" began to ply between Helensburgh, Greenock and Glasgow. Built at John Wood's Port Glasgow yard to the design of Henry Bell, a Helensburgh mill-wright hotel owner, it was not the first steam-boat to be constructed yet, as Marwick remarks, "its name is immortalised in the annals of the Clyde". Her first voyage, up-river to the Broomielaw, took an astonishing three and a half hours. Hitherto such journeys had been more extended and hazardous. Sailing from Glasgow, "the vehicles of communication to the port of Greenock were a species of wherry-built nutshells designated 'flyboats' [which] generally completed their voyage in the short space of ten hours! The conveyances of goods and passengers to places more remote were a more ambitious sort of machine, generally known by the name of 'Packet', which, with a fair wind, could reach the Isle of Bute in three days; but, when adverse, thought it 'not wonderful' to plough the billowy main for as many weeks!"

29 a distinctly 1930s block of shops and offices.

The key building of the grid, set in the town's first burial ground and anchored on the axis of Church Street, is **St Andrew's Church** (1823, refurbished 1898), a pavilion-roofed galleried kirk fronted by a pilastered pedimented facade from which rises a central belfry, classically conceived but of rather dumpy proportions. Serving Mammon, are the **Clydesdale Bank,** 39 Princes Street, and the **Royal Bank,** 49 Princes Street, both Victorian Renaissance *palazzi* in good ashlar. But by far the oldest and most interesting buildings in this part of town are **9** and **11 King Street.** Both are two storeys high, rubble-built and slated: 9 (1746) built as a Masonic Lodge, has a forestair at the rear; 11 (1758), which once served as the Town Hall, is longer and higher with quoined margins and a segmentally arched pend leading into the back court.

Beyond the gridded centre, linear development continues in several streets paralleling the contours and intermittently connected by short steep inclines. Cut off from the river by a dual carriageway, both Shore Street and Brown Street retain a rather frustrated sense of the esplanade — a feeling peculiarly pointed up by the replica of the diminutive *Comet* paddle steamer which perches daintily in a car-park pond, an imaginative *memorial to Henry Bell and the expertise of Port Glasgow craftsmen.* **St John's Church** (1854), high pinnacles rising from the four buttresses of its gable front, marks the start of a long slow curve which ends in the saddleback tower of John Burnet's Early Pointed, Arts and Crafts flavoured, **West Church** (1885). Beyond Jean Street is the **County Cinema** (c. 1935), Glasgow Road; now a bingo hall, its vertically stressed cream-tiled front has kept the bombast but none of the magic of its picture palace days.

Jean Street School
H. and D. Barclay (1883-84)
Another of the many school buildings which the Barclays designed over the final quarter of last century. Like their Clune Park School (*q.v.*) it uses pilastrades to unify and centralise the elevations. The whole is well detailed, majestically scaled and capped by generously wide eaves.

Jean Street School.

Burniston

Pirrit

Newark Parish Church
(1773-74)

Though this was not the first church to be built in
Port Glasgow, it is now the oldest — a typical
pavilion-roofed galleried rubble-built block. A
description in the First Statistical Account — *an
elegant house of worship* . . . carried out *in a style
superior to most kirks in Scotland* — takes local pride
too far, but it can at least boast a more dramatic siting
than most; there is much underbuilding and a boldly
ramped drive sweeps up from Glen Avenue. In
1920-22 a square apse containing a pipe organ was
built onto the west end but in 1935-38 this became a
chancel in more refurbishment — choir room, toilets,
chapel, etc. — by R. Mervyn Noad (chancel furniture
by Archibald Dawson). These changes, creating a
more spacious but less Presbyterian arrangement in
the interior, scarcely respected the austere symmetry
of the exterior.

Bolder departures from symmetry can be seen at
Glenpark, Glen Avenue, a standard pilastered and
pedimented late Georgian house vastly extended, most
dramatically on the south-east in a domed four-
storeyed bastion of tiered bay windows. Crisp ashlar
and fine carving contrast strongly with the cruder pink
stone of the old house, yet somehow this very quality
of detail and execution serves to mitigate the overall
effect of compositional imbalance. Since 1980 the
house has served as a home for the elderly — a fate
considerably preferable to death. Meanwhile, on
neighbouring **Ivybank**, a handful of pre-1850 villas
remain terminally indigent.

Newark Parish Church.

West Church, Brown Street.

RCAHMS

Customs House Quay, c. 1835; engraving by W. H. Bartlett and F. W. Topham.

Garvel Park House from south-east.

RCAHMS

CARTSDYKE

Port Glasgow merges into Greenock imperceptibly, the common legacy of a maritime industrial economy everywhere present. Between road and river the landscape of shipyards and docks, its skyline of mechanical tracery rising behind the leaden bulk of workshops and sheds, continues for more than two

71 miles. At the long brick **Warehouses** (1886) on East Hamilton Street, however, something of Greenock's greater investment and precedence becomes apparent — almost 700 feet of dockside polychromatic brickwork. Behind are **Garvel Graving Dock** (1871-74) and **James Watt Dock** (1878-86) both built to the design of Walter R. Kinipple when, as provost Abram Lyle said, *There had never in the history of Greenock been a more momentous time, involving greater interests or a greater outlay of money . . ..* The cost of James Watt Dock reached an astonishing £850,000.

72 **Garvel Park House**
(1777)
A dilapidated five-bay Georgian mansion, pedimented on each facade with a Corinthian columned doorpiece and urns to the south and Gothick astragals to the stair window on the north. Once the retreat of Baillie James Gammell, it was originally *out in the country* at the end of a long avenue in the midst of riparian

parkland. Now it is marooned incongruously in dockland.

It scarcely seems possible that this slummy industrial suburb of Cartsdyke (or Craufurdsdyke, as it was also known from the Craufurds of Kilbirnie who held Cartsburn estate from the 16th century) should once have been of greater maritime and mercantile importance than Greenock itself. Perhaps the fact that part of the disastrous Darien Expedition of 1697 set out from here was an ill omen for the community's future. All that recalls its past now is the curve of the old High Street where Main Street bends through the brick cliffs of the yards while further on, across Rue End Street from Joseph Locke's **Victoria Harbour** (1846-50) there is perhaps just a trace of the symmetrical street layout developed in pre-Victorian days around the vanished open space of St Andrew's Square. Little enough of Victorian Cartsdyke (from 1841 merged with Greenock) remains either, for much was destroyed in the blitz of May 1941 and most of the rest has since been cut away in re-development.

73   **Cartsdyke Parish Church** (1856) by Duncan McFarlane, *combining economy with elegance*, as *The Greenock Telegraph* said, still thrusts its little broach spire amongst the high-rise blocks of the '70s. There are a few undistinguished tenements, those at **Morton Terrace**, 2-9 Carwood Street (c. 1875), plain and straight but with a solid rough dignity. At East Crawfurd Street is a surprisingly English row of close-packed brick semis at **Octavia Cottages** (1866), built

Below Morton Terrace, c. 1900. **Bottom** Opening of Jas. Watt Dock, 1886. Inset are Robert Shankland, provost, and Thos. Wilson, secretary of the Harbour Trust. Garvel House is background left.

Inverclyde District Libraries

Illustrated London News

St Lawrence Church.

to enable *working men to become proprietors of their own houses.* The experiment failed and vast expanses of local authority housing cover the slopes above the riverside yards and docks, from the gabled and hipped roughcast cottages of the early 1920s to fifteen-storey panel-clad point blocks.

74 Amongst all this rootless modernism, **Elliot Court** (1982) on Carwood Street, by Drew Forbes, stands out — a modest and highly successful attempt to preserve the streetline but vary the skyline. More arrogant, but worth a look, are two churches on Bawhirley Road: the **East Congregational Church** (1968) by Fred McDermid, a squat composition of dull-red brick boxes lit by hefty monopitch rooflights and Gillespie, 75 Kidd and Coia's **St Lawrence Church** (1951-54) at the foot of Kilmacolm Road; redder bricks this time, its high roof section repeated in a series of triangular windows to clerestorey and chancel.

Customs House.

GREENOCK TOWN CENTRE

Of the several harbours which indented the shoreline from the debouch of the Delling Burn to the Bay of Quick, only the **East India Harbour** (1805-09) by John Rennie, remains. The **West Harbour** (1707-10), the town's first, constructed to combat the threatening dominance of Glasgow's nearby Port, has been filled in; so, too, has the great basin which Bell and Miller created to form **Albert Harbour** (1862-67), while, farthest west, **Princes Pier** (1862-70), shorn of its playful towered and tiled station buildings, now completes the transformation into the Clydeport Container Terminal.

76 **Custom House**
William Burn (1818)
A single magnificent building to recall the great days:
a high ashlar palace, classically severe, with a massive
Doric entablature and attic parapet all round. A
pedimented portico projects on the main riverside
front, aligned with the tall cast-iron **Beacon
Fountain** — Corinthian column, clock, beacon light
and weather vane — which local marine artist William
Clark designed for the quay in 1868. A second
portico, on the east side, marks the entrance to the
Excise Department. It is all the most substantial
architectural measure of bygone trade.

Close encounters with the river are rare: fishing is
a casual quayside activity now, not the herring
klondike it was two centuries ago when perhaps a
hundred and fifty boats sailed out into the Firth; and
the big ships are seldom seen, though the tugs packed
into Victoria Harbour still bring nautical excitement
right up to the edge of Rue End Street. Some of the
old vennels remain — evocative names like
Drummers' Close and **Mince Collop Close,** but
little more.

William Street, however, leading directly into
Cathcart Square, has kept just a flavour of its original
character. The three-storeyed property at **9** (1752) is a
great tenement, Greenock's oldest surviving residential
building (restored by Boswell, Mitchell and Johnston).
Next door, on the corner, was the birthplace of the
town's most famous son, James Watt (1736-1819), an
77 event marked by the **Watt Memorial School** (1908),
a Scots Renaissance exercise by H. and D. Barclay;
cap house tower, turrets and pedimented dormers all
well detailed, but the corner is gauchely turned with
an internal angle in which sits H. C. Fehr's
pedestalled bronze statute of the great man. **10
William Street** (1755) is again rehabilitated original;
a low residential building whose street facade has a
bold curvilinear gable known locally as the *Dutch
Gable.*

78 **Mid Kirk**
(1759-61; refurbished 1878)
The church dominates the still-causeyed space of
Cathcart Square (c. 1750). Known at first as the
New Kirk, since demand for a second place of
worship besides the Old West Kirk had been clamant
in the town and *nothing would settle the people . . . but
following forth the design of building the church*, it is a
five-bay pavilion-rooofed, galleried hall enhanced on
the north by a pedimented portico in Roman Ionic.
The noble facade design may have been obtained by
Sir John Schaw from Bristol though he had certainly
instructed that the dimensions of the earlier parish

Below 10 William Street.
Bottom Watt Memorial School,
looking up William Street to the
Mid Kirk.

Inverclyde District Libraries

Inverclyde District Libraries

117

church at Port Glasgow be taken before building in Greenock began. The *city church* interior is broad and galleried on three sides with a coved ceiling. In 1787 the steeple, its base already embedded within the church behind the portico, was finally raised in four stages to a height of 146 feet.

79 **Municipal Buildings**
H. and D. Barclay (1879-86)
The Mid Kirk's steeple, however, is still 100 feet short of the dome on the **Victoria Tower** which rose a century or so later, at the north-west corner of Cathcart Square, a point of orientation for miles around whether from land or sea. This profligate height and the sheer size and decorative richness of the town's civic buildings testify even more conspicuously than the great harbour projects to Greenock's 19th century wealth. But not everyone was impressed. As one shipowner put it in 1888, *every beauty but the beauty of economy has been studied in the erection of the Municipal Buildings.* The architects who won the commission in competition with more than eighty others, achieved a complex design drenched in classical detail and sculpture, with lavishly garnished interiors, skilfully enclosing an older building and adjusting the composition of plan and elevation to the

Municipal Buildings with Cowan's Corner in the foreground and Hamilton Street to the left.

There is *an ironical, even incredible ring to James Watt's remark that "the Scots were naturally incapable of becoming engineers". Nonetheless, the truth is that, in 1764, having found that the efficiency of the Newcomen steam engine might be transformed by the introduction of a separate condenser, he was forced to realise his invention with English technology. In Birmingham, Boulton and Watt produced the engines that began to power the Industrial Revolution.*

Despite Watt's scepticism, in lowland Scotland engineering became a national pursuit — in the mines and textile mills, on the railways, and — most significantly for Watt's home town of Greenock — on the high seas.

RCAHMS

118

perimeter of a large irregular plot. Except, that is, at
the south-east corner close to the tower! There, from
the beginning, one proprietor held out against all
blandishment. As a result, the loggia of shops on the
south side of the site, which originally ran along
Hamilton Street and now faces Clyde Square,
remained incomplete. Wartime bombing destroyed the
frustrating tenement on Cowan's Corner, but the gap
is still there articulating — by default — the open turn
west out of Cathcart Square.

Clyde Square, first envisaged in the 1940s, did
not come into existence until 1975 though
improvements in this part of the town centre had
started in the 1930s with clearances in the crowded
Long Vennel area. The square gains immeasurably
from the Barclays' ornate arcaded facade. Opposite is
the slate-clad box of the **Library** (1970) by Burgh
Architect James Watson; placed on a raised terrace, its
book-end fenestration draws a striated curtain along
the south side of the Square. Below and between, the
levels split and change, leading west into the new
pedestrianised shopping *streets* of Hamilton Way and
Hamilton Gate. Display windows and passers-by catch
the eye here, not buildings — which, perhaps, is just
as well. Nevertheless, there is some good two-tone
brick housing to be found at **Westburn Street** and
Charles Court (1975), all solidly Dutch in feel, by
Hugh Martin and Partners.

Although the transition between Cathcart Square
and Clyde Square is unsatisfactorily open, each space
has its own pronounced identity. Both have
centrepieces: one, a long fibreglass sculpture of
shipyard workers hauling a ship's propeller, a design
by Naomi Hunt and Malcolm Robertson (1975) based
on one of Stanley Spencer's war-time drawings; the
other, F. A. Scudamore's **Lyle Fountain** (1880), a
lacy cast iron cage bearing the crests of eighteen of
Greenock's leading families.

Cathcart Street has a series of respectable bank
buildings. James Salmon, mixing arched and
lintelled windows, respectfully designed his **British
Linen Bank,** 4 Cathcart Street, with some attention
to Baird and Thomson's **Greenock Provident Bank**
(1861-62), now the T.S.B. round the corner at 11
William Street. The **Clydesdale Bank** (1900-01), also
by Baird and Thomson, maintains the high scale but
changes from ochre to red sandstone and steps up the
decorative elaboration. Next, the **Royal Bank**
(c. 1875), formerly the National Commercial, also rich
in detail with consoles, eaves cornice and a massive
balcony which, for no good reason, overlooks the
narrow alley of Cross Shore Street. Then the **Post
Office** (1898-99), a fairly typical Renaissance facade
by W. W. Robertson and the Office of Works, with a

Below Municipal Buildings, Clyde
Square facade.
Bottom Clydesdale Bank, Cathcart
Square.

Inverclyde District Libraries

Inverclyde District Libraries

*"**During** the day the town channels mind and eye swiftly out to the river and the hills, constantly transcending self by the dynamics of its construction. It is only in the evenings, and especially in the autumnal early nights that it states itself. Then the sky takes on a steely blue clarity and against this in edges of unbearable blue black the buildings inflict themselves, the simplicity of outline fantasticated by the chimney abstractions, castles, chess problems, graveside gatherings, with the smoke in slow upgoing to the enormous empty sky.*

At this time there is a heroism in the shapes and the colours, an elemental starkness which attains archetype, a town looking across a river at the hills. The river flows, the hills abide and the town ponders these images of evanescence and antiquity, while above, with the disinterest of the truly eternal, the sky endures."

(From Sharp, A., A Green Tree in Gedde, Joseph, London, 1967 (1965), p. 9.)

1-5 Shaw Place with 5-7 Bank Street to left.

central open gablet flanked by mansard dormers. Of the two original Ionic entrances only the left, with Victoria's head above, still functions; the other has been closed and Albert replaced by a clock. Finally, with something of the bleak emptiness of a re-built East European town, the far end of Cathcart Street

81 opens at **Cathcart Buildings** into a broad, almost symmetrical, space in front of Central Station. Frank Burnet and Bell's four-storey brick and ashlar housing (1955-57) is certainly dull, but not without the haunting heavy-handed *naïveté* of the time.

South of Cathcart Street the land rises abruptly. Perched on the hillside are some of Greenock's earliest buildings. At **5-7 Bank Street** (1810-11) — not surprisingly perhaps — yet another bank; the original premises of the Renfrewshire Bank with a splendid horseshoe stair climbing up from street level to a high

82 porch. Across the street is **Shaw Place,** a line of five flatted Georgian town houses (c. 1830-35, **no. 4** c. 1815) packed together in terrace formation. All are three windows wide with pilastered or columned doorways in Roman Doric, with the exception of two which are somewhat grander. Similar early houses, frequently flatted — common throughout Greenock — occur in the streets behind, e.g. at **41** and **46 Regent Street** and **5-9 Roxburgh Street** while at **Abbotsford Place,** 11-15 Roxburgh Street, and **21 Bank Street** the metamorphosis of the flatted Georgian block into Victorian tenement is begun.

RCAHMS

120

Inverclyde District Libraries

Well Park is reached along the terraced walks east
of Bank Street. Here overseeing the town, was Lord
Cathcart's *auld castell-heid, castle, tour, fortalice and
manor place, etc. new built* in 1635. This **Mansion
House,** demolished in 1886 during railway tunnelling,
MacGibbon and Ross were able to document fully,
describing it as *a picturesque assemblage of crow-stepped
gables and chimneys, which were evidently the work of
various periods* including by then a rather gaunt 18th
century wing said to have been built for the Schaws in
1740 by James Watt *père*. Nothing now remains save
83 the **Well** (1629), and some gate piers (c. 1635). On the
terraced hillside, stood the house of the Baron Bailie
who, from 1635 until the creation of a Town Council
in 1751, administered local government on the Laird's
behalf.

84 **Well Park Church**
J., J. M. and W. H. Hay (1853-54)
Designed in a revived Decorated style it has a
powerfully buttressed and pinnacled spire surging over
the west end entrance, pyramid roofed stair towers in
the internal angles at the transepts and a clever
transition into three storeys of hall accommodation at
the east. Since 1979, faith in its future has gone and
the vandals have turned it into a burnt-out shell with
little hope.

Below former Mansion House.
Bottom Well Park Church.

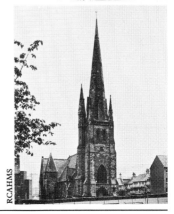

RCAHMS

I

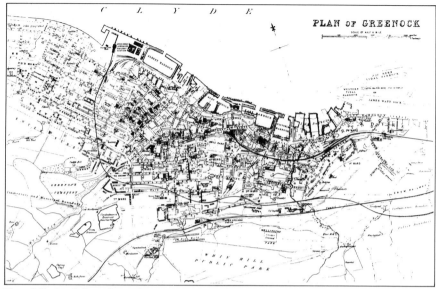

Plan of Greenock from Groome's
Gazetteer, 1882-85.

THE GREENOCK GRIDS

South of Well Park the rectilinear disposition of the
streets begins to reveal that planned expansion which
Greenock undertook around the turn of the 18th into
the 19th century. At least two plans were prepared
prior to 1800; one c. 1780, probably by a surveyor
named Richardson; the other *A Plan of the New Town
of Greenock* by the Edinburgh architect William
Sibbald (?-1809). Further plans by a Kilwinning
surveyor, A. Kenneth, record the growth of the town
up to 1807 but do not break new ground. In 1818,
however, there appeared a *Plan of the Town of
Greenock and its Environs, with the Intended
Improvements by David Reid*, a comprehensive
proposal covering the estates of Greenock and
Cartsdyke and determining, in effect, the final layout
of the modern town. So admired has it been that, over
a century later, during the promotion of the Greenock
Burgh Extension Bill of 1927, it was described in the
House of Commons as *one of the best in the world*.
This may be pitching things too high for what is, after
all, no more than a series of straightforward grids, but
certainly the generous plots and broad streets of the
West End, combining as they do with spectacular
views over the Firth to the Dunbartonshire hills, have
proved a salubrious and enviable legacy.

Reid's plan shows that the growth of Greenock
would follow four distinct grid alignments disposed
around the older central core behind the quays. As in
Glasgow, the contiguity of adjacent grids with
differing orientation, the presence of a few more
casual routes emerging from the irregular patterns of

David Reid *remains a shadowy
figure. He was certainly a brother of
the Rev. Archibald Reid, who
prepared the entry for Greenock
Parish in the First Statistical
Account of 1793, but a tempting
relationship with Robert Reid
(1774-1856) "King's Architect and
Surveyor in Scotland", who had been
associated with Sibbald in planning
the first extension of Edinburgh's
New Town in 1802, is without
substantiation.*

the old town or developed in response to some contingent quirkiness in feuing, and, of course, above all, the scenic implications of a constantly rising topography, all lent variety and interest to the evolving townscape.

Expansion had to be south and west. A grid based on the crossing of Lynedoch Street and Regent Street, for example, runs from the Delling Burn as far as Bank Street. Beyond Bank Street, a second network of four closely parallel streets extended as far as the West Burn and the oblique line of the old Inverkip Road. This grid, lying south of Roxburgh Street, is deliberately elongated east-west since the incline to the south is now steeper. Elongated, too, is a third layout of streets to the north-west of the old town centre on the other side of the West Burn. This more downtown quarter, centred on West Blackhall Street was already foreshadowed in the 1780 plan and so from an early date it was built up rapidly. Finally comes the West End, by far the grandest and most extensive of Greenock's grids, its controlling geometry anticipated by Sibbald at the right-angled junction of Nelson Street and Union Street where new was hinged to old at Kiblain Square. This slightly canted irregular open space, soon known as George Square, remains *the main gateway to the New Town.*

The Lynedoch Street Grid

The grid based on **Lynedoch Street** is essentially tenemental. Only its western half, however, remains. 85 **25-35 Regent Street** (c. 1870) is typical; three plain storeys of shops and flats and an almost intact series of regular attic bays each neatly slated round its half-cone roof. Trim little dormers like these crop up time after time in Greenock; they cannot be bettered. From **6-74 Lynedoch Street** sporadic *improvements* to the long roofscape are particularly unfortunate since an overall elevational coherence is more or less maintained with wide pedimented gable-ends symmetrically flanking the street junctions of the grid. **Lyle Street's** tenements have unusually high doorways with pilasters elongated or raised inelegantly in order to incorporate light to the first landing of the common stair above — a co-ordinated solution repeatedly favoured in Greenock. Quite unique, however, are conversions at **1a, 1b** and **1c Hope Street** in which a combination of varied floor levels, canted oriels and forestairs produces an unexpectedly agitated intrusion in the tenement walls. Otherwise there is almost nothing to break the strong sense of containment. Even Rennison and Scott's **Wellpark West Church** (1877) on Regent Street — a big unbuttressed box — keeps this addiction to the wall plane.

*"**The cluster** of old tenements on the hill, the long latitudinals, Holmscroft, Wellington, Dempster and the steep cross gridding of Bank Street and Trafalgar Street, then Ann Street and Mount Pleasant, an area of stone and smoke, chimney capped, long high canyons diced with windows and old women cushioned on the sills. Glimpses into kitchens hung with holy pictures and tinted soldiers dead in their frames. . . . A soft flaking world of stone and soot shot through by surprising lances at the river and the hills."*

(From Sharp, A., A Green Tree in Gedde, Joseph, London, 1967 (1965), p. 25.)

Grid-iron townscape in the West End.

RCAHMS

Walker

Regent Street.

Highlanders' Academy.

Walker

James Watt (1736-1819) does not lack commemorative monuments in Greenock: the Watt Museum and Library housing the scientific library which he himself had founded in 1816, the great dock at Garvel Park opened in 1886 bearing his name, the Watt Memorial College built in 1908 on the site of his birthplace in William Street. But the greatest monument of all, conceived in 1854 as a tower 289 feet high to be constructed with stone brought from all over the world, remained unbuilt.

Memorial Tower proposed in honour of James Watt.

The Southern Grid

The transition from the first to the second of Greenock's grids occurs across the irregular blocks bounded by Bank Street and Mearns Street. At the east end of **Roxburgh Street** is a second generation group of red sandstone properties erected by Greenock Central Co-operative Society: at **16-24**, four richly carved storeys of shops and flats (1893) by W. Burns Stewart; at **23**, a three-storey and mansard block (1904) by Boston, Menzies and Morton, with a wide *Art Nouveau* eaves cornice; at **8-14** a lower office building (1914) with strongly horizontal cornices and parapet; and, round the corner in Mearns Street, its later continuation still in red sandstone, but fluted and facetted in hefty cinema Moderne idiom — evidently it paid dividends to move with the stylistic trends.

Armadale Terrace would be unremarkable but for its *Art Nouveau* close tiles, but **18-20 Mearns Street** (1906), vigorously modelled in a rude Edwardian Baroque, is anything but perfunctory. None of this is original but it is at least streetwise. A few blocks west, however, housing varies from eighteen- to two-storeys, streets cease to be perceptible space and a system-built **Health Centre** (1980-81) by Lane, Bremner and Garnett looks just as incongruous as the dual-doored Star of David gable of Pilkington and Bell's **Mount Park Free Church** (1874) now does, washed up on Trafalgar Street above this flood of renewal.

Wellington Street and **Dempster Street** recall the older order — particularly towards their east and west ends where vestiges of the original three-storey tenement corridors remain. Facades are severely plain; a genuine street architecture which, with its raised ground floor storeys and stilted close-mouth doorways, is unmistakably Greenock. The dull mass of **Mearns Street School** (1875) fits the austere architectural mould and though the ornate Renaissance detail and arcading of David Barclay's **Highlanders' Academy** (1886-87) does not, its high playground walls do respect the street grid. Ironically, where the grid begins to break down along **Murdieston Street**, the tenements continue with only slight adaptation and variation, curving downhill to reach the oblique line of the Old Inverkip Road.

The Inverkip Road

At the beginning of the 19th century the ancient road coming over the hill from Inverkip followed the West Burn down into the centre of Greenock. Reid, of course, retained this route in his proposals. In effect, it bisected the angle formed between the Roxburgh Street grid and the West End.

On the north side of **Brachelston Square**, the right-angled junction of South Street and Nelson Street anchors and defines the grid-iron logic of the

90 West End plan. Through Charles Wilson's **Cemetery Gates** (1847), however, is a romantic landscape of free-flowing paths winding languidly uphill among the tombs. Set in this *other world* in an open grove amidst the trees, the stiff forms of Cullen, Lochead and

91 Brown's **Crematorium** (1959) are — as is so often the case with such buildings — an insipid celebration of death. But search a little more, for there are things here to touch the heart, like the Neoclassical *tristesse* of Mossman's **Highland Mary Monument** (1842) or, mourning for architecture itself, a crumbling **Tempietto** summer house (c. 1830), shamefully neglected behind prim high hedges.

South of the square, the streets are again built up: tenements (c. 1875) from **Brachelston Street** to **Nicholson Street**; the frivolous parapetted front of Neil Duff's **La Scala** (1913) on Inverkip Street, less decorated now than scruffily shed-like; and two imposingly contrived churches.

92 **Orangefield Baptist Church**
Thomas McLelland (1877)
Elevated above a basement storey of hall accommodation, it gains extra height, accenting its presence in a single pinnacle rising above the corner like an exclamation mark.

93 **St Patrick's Church**
Gillespie, Kidd and Coia (1935)
No less assertive with its soaring red brick gable behind which four pairs of high brick dormers punch through the mansardic section of the nave roof. A certain fussiness is present, partly the result of a cramped plot and littled helped by an undue attention to the plumbing, but the bold industrial redness of the brick, complemented throughout by Archibald Dawson's exquisite stone sculpture, makes no concessions and the fundamental tectonic strength of Jack Coia's design is undiminished.

From Orangefield, Inverkip Road skirts the cemetery hill below the ungainly fish tank box of the

94 **McNeil Memorial Baths** (1966) before curving out through Greenock's endless periphery of housing. Past **Ravenscraig Hospital** (1876-79), a Baronial

RCAHMS

Inverclyde District Libraries

Top Highland Mary's grave.
Above Summer House Tempietto.

IBM

IBM in Spango Valley.

spread in red, by John Starforth, the road runs into Spango Valley. IBM have been eating up the landscape — but not without style! The tanned transparency of two silky-smooth **Office Blocks** (1971, 1977), by Matthews, Ryan and Partners, could scarcely be more sophisticated, nor the vast bland bulk of the latest computerised **Distribution Centre** (1981), by Robert Matthew, Johnson-Marshall and Partners, more suavely ascetic.

In the opposite direction, Inverkip Street heads back into the centre of town. On the right a high rubble wall screens the old **Graveyard** which served Greenock from 1786 until the cemetery was opened further west in 1846; above the plain portal is a reminder that John Galt (1779-1839) *forerunner of the realistic movement in Scottish fiction*, is buried here.

Downhill the old route is lost, overlaid by the new roads, service yards and shopping streets west of Clyde Square. A truncated cylinder — the roof of the **Rotunda Pub** (1972) — pops up like a funnel above the bustle at the foot of Kilblain Street but, apart from this symbolic gesture, there is no intimation of the river. Nor is there anything to suggest that hereabouts ran the course of the West Burn.

The North-West Grid

Westburn Street marks the short southern edge of the third of Greenock's grids; the one which, closest to harbours and town centre, antedates the others in terms of dense urban build-up. The three principal streets run north-south.

Dalrymple Street has little to offer. Here, however, at the foot of Nicolson Street on the shoreside, close to the mouth of the West Burn, stood the **Old West Kirk** of 1591. One of the earliest post-Reformation churches in Scotland, its construction

95

In 1811, *a certain William Peebles, who had three times been satirised by Burns, attempted to extract some revenge by an attack on Greenock Burns Club. Unable to abide the thought of Burns becoming a national celebrity, he mocked the enthusiasms engendered by the bard's Greenock devotees (the Club was the first to be formally constituted in 1801), ridiculing how they had*
". . . from age to age,
As for a monarch, hero, sage,
Let anniversaries repeat
His glories, celebrate a fete
Imbibe his spirit, sing his songs,
Extol his name, lament his
wrongs,
His death deplore, accuse his fate
And raise this name far above the
great
What call you this? Is it Insania?
I'll coin a word, 'tis Burnomania,
His Greenock friends we therefore
dub
The Annual Burnomanian Club."

was authorised by a Royal Charter granted by James VI in 1589. But, repeatedly altered and enlarged, condemned in 1837, rebuilt in 1864 by James Salmon, and more and more engulfed by shipbuilding, it was finally demolished stone by stone in the early 1920s in order to make more room for a shipyard. Thereafter it was translated to its present site at Seafield at the foot of Campbell Street (*q.v.*).

West Blackhall Street keeps its cobbled surface and Victorian enclosure, but it has few buildings of quality. Best are two tenement blocks: **Lorne Court** and, across the street, **nos. 77-93**. Reverting to pre-Victorian small-town scale, **Grey Place House** (c. 1840), 131 West Blackhall Street, is rubble-built with plain margins and two typically Greenock attic dormers. **Grey Place**, which bends left to reach Brougham Street and the edge of the West End, presents a varied line of these same gable-to-gable houses (c. 1840-50), most with similar dormers (especially fine at **19-21**) and some with their original early Victorian shopfronts. Across the street through neo-Grec gatepiers (1857) is James Dempster's former
96 **St Columba's Gaelic Church** (1823), a tough classical box with high arched windows and a false portico of twinned Ionic columns above the ground floor entrance.

West Stewart Street is ageing, sad and confused. At its southern end, where things are busy and urban, a large supermarket and its attendant multi-level car park dominate the scene not so much by scale as by an aggressive repetition of blank horizontality. The
97 decorative dignities of John Henderson's **St Andrew's Church** (1835-36) have been all but concealed in placarded banalities. Henderson, a pupil of Thomas Hamilton, *made Gothic his special study* and although this church may not have been the equal of others he built in the east, the quality of the Tudor Gothic detail of two ogee-hooded windows set beneath a corbelled oriel on the Argyle Street side of the
98 church can still be enjoyed. **St John's Masonic Temple** (1897) has not been interfered with but its red sandstone has eroded badly; nonetheless, Boston Menzies and Morton are as always marvellously inventive. The same dubious stone must have been used by J. B. Stewart for his **Struthers Memorial Church** (1896), formerly the Reformed Presbyterian, for the Gothicised mouldings have also decayed. Here the street too disintegrates. The red brick of Burnet, Bell and Partners' **Stewart House** (1982), a flatted development of three stepped monopitches is well groomed, yet with a raddled look of almost desperate renewal. Perhaps it is better than nothing, but hardly fair exchange for the Venetian-windowed mansions that once graced this unfortunate street.

Top St Columba's Gaelic Church.
Above St John's Masonic Temple.

When, in 1769, *John Wilson*, "*a poet of considerable merit*", became schoolmaster at the local grammar school, the Magistrates instructed him to abandon his "profane" art. Repining at this inhibition, Wilson wrote to his son "I once thought to live by the breath of fame, but how miserably was I disappointed when, instead of having only performances applauded in crowded theatres, and being caressed by the great — for what will not a poetaster in his intoxicated delirium of possession dream? — I was condemned to bawl myself to hoarseness to wayward brats . . . the contempt of shopkeepers and brutish skippers." Clearly the Muse was much less warmly entertained in Greenock than in neighbouring Paisley.

THE WEST END

99 **George Square**'s location was already determined by 1790. Yet more than a generation later it was still open country. The 1832 Parliamentary Boundary Plan of Greenock shows only a few isolated buildings occupying what is clearly intended as the principal approach to the prestigious West End. Over the next half century, however, expansion accelerated.

The early residential character of the Square is still evident. On the west are three tenements (c. 1830) with turnpike stairs at the rear, their elevations varying in decorative inflection — shallow pediment, tri-partite window, recessed pilastered doorway. **5** and **6 George Square** (c. 1835) are more upmarket, the former with a central doorway distinguished by concave reveals and a charming square-headed fanlight. This mixture of tenement and detached town house proved to be the pattern of 19th century development throughout the West End. George Square, however, with a very Victorian coincidence of ultimate values and planning decorum soon became more ecclesiastical than residential.

Below George Square Baptist Church.
Bottom St George's North Church.

Inverclyde District Libraries

George Square Congregational Church
John Baird I (1839-40)
Pinnacled Perpendicular: if it is the *standard firescreen-gabled west front* (here facing south), this is not surprising since Baird was instructed to follow *a Gothic entrance elevation drawn in pencil* by a member of the congregation.

George Square Baptist Church
James Sellars (1888)
Plain yet restlessly disturbed by Baroque allusions, licentious enough to have urns on a split pediment. This is Sellars, by now *badly overworked* and a long way from his Neoclassical best.

Inverclyde District Libraries

100 ### St George's North Church
Salmon Son and Ritchie (1870-71)
Built as the Middle U.F., round-arched and stiffly Renaissance, its great asset is a tall tower standing above the long axis of Union Street, its impact surely the result of more than a passing acquaintance with William Stark's St George's Tron Steeple in Glasgow. The original interior has been destroyed by fire.

Nelson Street, connecting George Square with Brachelston Square, defines the south-eastern boundary of the West End grid. The wide carriageway sets the tone for the disciplined but leisurely streets beyond. Not so the architecture which is heterogeneous in building type, materials and style. Fortunately, quality is not lacking.

101 Sheriff Court
Peddie and Kinnear (1864-67)

Sheriff Court illustrated in *The Builder*.

A spikey mass of symmetrical Baronial. Three gabled dormers and a bartizan jut above a heavily modelled corbel course on either side of a central tower in which these same features are compressed into a steep and agitated pyramid. On the end elevations the two parallel pitched roofs needed to cover a large square plan appear as crow-step gables between which a high chimney stack is trapped; again, a compositional procedure imploded in the lateral elevations of the tower. There is more than a hint of the almost contemporary Morgan Academy, Dundee, also by Peddie and Kinnear, in all this. Greenock, however, is more compact and altogether less exuberant: early fears that *the front Elevation would be more expensive than was necessary* may not have gone unheeded. The ashlar walls of a single-storey court building added alongside by the PSA architects in 1980-81, are even more austerely plain — though much enlivened by bold chamfering of sills and plinths.

Old Kirk.

102 Old Kirk
David Cousin (1839-41)

Pointedly placed on the axis of Brisbane Street, the church is five bays long, each lit by a tall, arched window, end bays being emphasised by twinned pilasters, entablature and balustraded parapet. The street facade repeats the twinned pilaster theme on each side of the projecting central tower from which a

Walker

Formerly, and rather confusingly, known as the New West Kirk, the old Kirk came into existence following the Presbytery's closure of the Old West Kirk after the congregation there had raised a petition in 1835 complaining of the unhealthy state of their 16th century building: the ancient "churchyard was so filled up that the earth outside was two feet above the level of the floor, and in rainy weather it was necessary to place boards to enable the people to step in at the doors". Once inside, indeed, the worshippers found themselves "sitting over a pool of liquid mud".

slender Wren-like steeple (1854-55) rises through five stages, two of which have coupled angle columns. In the belfry is the original bell of 1677 taken from the Old West Kirk. In 1912 the interior of the church was gutted, refurbished and a chancel added by John Keppie. Until recently the right hand side of Nelson Street began in good classical style. Demolition has, however, removed a fine Scottish Georgian house. Beyond, restoration has favoured something more incongruous, whimsical and English: James B. Stewart's red brick **Ardgowan Hospice**, formerly the Eye Infirmary (1893), is a Free Style cottage with hints of Norman Shaw. Stewart's **Ardgowan School** (1896) prefers texture and polychromy to decorative

103 elaboration. **James Watt College** (1973) by Boissevain and Osmond is even more abstemious; cool and well-calculated, the acceptable face of Modernism. Eight-storeys may be thought too many for this part of town but the plot, formerly the site of the original Greenock Academy of 1855, is big, and the building's high and low massing respects the orthogonal layout of the streets. Detailing is crisp and minimal but not paper-thin, and the proportions have a stylish American zest.

Union Street runs north-west from George Square through Ardgowan Square taking the shorter high road to Gourock. The scenic advantages of the shoreside route, initially based on Brougham Street, had prime appeal but it was not long before Union Street, too, attracted development. Many early 19th century mansions remain; two-storey three-bay ashlar houses, small but elegant with a pleasant variety in porches and doorpieces. **12-22 Union Street** form an

104 attractive group. **17 Jamaica Street**, which presents a gable and the rear stair to its upper flat to Union Street, has rubble walls with in-and-out rusticated quoins which make a late 18th century date probable.

Union Church (1834), by John Baird I, maintains classical restraint with a severely plain pilastered and pedimented front. But there are departures. **St John's Episcopal Church** (1877-78), which replaced James Dempster's earlier adjacent building of 1824-25, is an orthodox nave-and-aisles plan with no transepts, distinguished more by the quality of its square-snecked rubble masonry than by the mildly decorated Gothic idiom of its North of England Anglican architects, Paley and Austin. It seems more than likely that its abruptly terminated tower is a failure of nerve or money.

Inverclyde District Libraries

Watt Library
105 Edward Blore (1835-46)
A three-storey collegiate building in bayed and battlemented English Tudor, it sits back from the

Top James Watt College.
Above St John's Episcopal Church.

street behind a balustraded garden wall. The composition is symmetrical, a pinnacled porch leading directly into a galleried reading room on the main axis of which sits Sir Francis Chantrey's white marble statue (c. 1840) of James Watt. Later extensions adding a hall and museum (1876) were successfully effected by A. Adamson in similar style.

106 **Ardgowan Square,** unlike the contemporary development of Blythswood Square in Glasgow's Second New Town, has developed without effective design control. The square itself, somewhat cluttered by hedges, bowling green and tennis courts, does not provide the spatial clarity it should, while the surrounding buildings add up to an interesting but incoherent aggregation. This weakness in the whole is regrettable, but by no means disastrous, for the parts, or some of them, have their own individual architectural quality. **29** is a typical two-storey three-bay house (c. 1830) with Ionic columned doorpiece. **30** is similar but earlier (c. 1815), with a Roman Doric door. Grander in every sense than these is **The Greenock Club** (1867-69), a square porched Italian Renaissance *palazzo* by Boucher and Cousland, with vermiculated quoins and window surrounds and a heavily ornate eaves cornice. At **2** and **3 Union Street** it is the mixture as before: relatively modest classical houses (c. 1840).

Top left Watt Library interior with Chantrey's statue of James Watt.
Top 12 Union Street.
Middle 9 Ardgowan Square.
Above 29 Ardgowan Square.

The Greenock Club.

Right Mansion House.

Pirrit

107 **The Mansion House**
R. Rowand Anderson (1886)
Built to accommodate the estate offices of the Shaw-Stewart family when the old Mansion House at Well Park (*q.v.*) was demolished, it has a wide palatial facade with a pavilion roof piended over projecting end bays and a semi-circular pediment over the central entrance block. Superficially orthodox in symmetrical 17th century Scots manner, it has also been infected — here one might better say diseased — by an incipient Baronial bug!

108 **The Tontine Hotel**
(1808)
It was George Robertson, a senior magistrate in the town with a considerable income derived from the Newfoundland trade, who created this the finest mansion in Greenock. The ground floor is rusticated but linked in plain ashlar quadrants to single-storey pavilion wings. Upper floors have architraved windows, the whole elevation, pedimented over a minimally defined three bay centre, delicately finished with a Greek fret frieze. The rear, also symmetrical, has bowed bays through all floors except the second where segmental balconies therefore occur. In 1892 the proprietor of the original Tontine Hotel in Cathcart Street (a grander but by no means dissimilar building which, like the Tontine in Ayr, had been built in 1802-03 to the design of John Paterson of Edinburgh) moved to Ardgowan Square and, retaining the hotel name, commenced business in Robertson's house. Some years later the rather busily glazed square porch was added, concealing the original doorpiece.

The rest of the Square has nothing comparable: more late Georgian houses; a muscular Thomsonesque villa with channelled quoins and wide eaves at **11**; a few tenements, **no. 8** in red sandstone with *Art Nouveau* tiles and stained glass.

Throughout Greenock's West End, a pattern of

Tontine Hotel.

RCAHMS

wide often tree-lined street prevails. Residential development predominates but there is no consistent commitment to a single housing type. Nevertheless, few streets are without examples of those elegant suburban mansions which Greenock's merchants and shipbuilders erected during the early years of last century.

Union Street has many. Elsewhere, too, they are liberally spread. Three in a row can be seen at 4-8 Brougham Street, all with Ionic door-pieces. 37 Campbell Street is similar but with a short flying stair across the area. Pavilion-roofed and more refined, Thornhill, 37 Ardgowan Street, has a broad tripartite window overarched in a blind segment on either side of a narrow Roman Doric porch. This was the family home of Hamish McCunn (1868-1916) that *most Scottish of Scottish composers.* Willowpark, 45 Ardgowan Street, has an unusual unfluted Greek Doric porch and single-storey quadrants. Almost out of sight, is Greenbank House, off Kelly Street, wide-fronted with tripartite windows and stepped parapets concealing its pavilion roof. More farm than mansion 109 perhaps, 151-155 Finnart Street is a plain two-storey gabled house given extra dignity by a central pediment with bull's eye motif and two single-storey pavilion wings both similarly pedimented, that to the right, still with its heavy Venetian window. Glenpark House, 48 Forsyth Street, now a teachers' centre, has a twin-columned Ionic porch beneath a two-bay pediment.

Inverclyde District Libraries

Inverclyde District Libraries

Top 4 Brougham Street.
Above 6 Brougham Street.

151-155 Finnart Street.

RCAHMS

Seafield Cottage, 48 Eldon Street.

Beyond the grid, strung out along the Low Gourock Road the late Georgian pattern continues. **Seafield Cottage**, 48 Eldon Street, which has a shallow pavilion roof with a wide bow-fronted facade and decorative ironwork porch to the Firth, and **84 Eldon Street**, in Batty Langley Gothick, are both single-storey but, on the large plots which originally ran down to the waterside and are now bounded by 110 the **Esplanade**, there are several two-storey mansions from this period, e.g. **19, 23** and **24.**

The **Esplanade** did not appear in Reid's 1818 plan. Instead, a wide crescent curved around, and in part across, the Bay of Quick. But, although this was tentatively begun in the east, it was never completed. In 1857 a new plan, drawn up by Glasgow engineers Bell and Miller, *for turning to account the mass of excavations from the ground on which Albert Harbour was being built* outlined a long and remarkably broad Esplanade running from Seafield to the Battery at Fort Matilda. Work was begun in 1863 and completed four years later.

Later villas break away from the disciplined symmetries of the original late Georgian models. Most lie in the extreme west end of the town beyond the limit of Reid's grid, i.e. beyond Glenpark cricket 111 ground. Sited above sloping lawns, **47 Eldon Street** (c. 1835 and later) is a big and bulbous asymmetrical pile, lightened by the Regency ironwork of its verandahs. There are towered Italianate mansions: **12 Newark Street** (c. 1860), **189 Eldon Street** (c. 1880) and, most Thomsonesque in detail, **213 Finnart Street.** Elizabethan has been tried too: **Madeira Lodge** (c. 1840) 16 Newark Street, is in plain rubble,

12 Newark Street.

but the much later, **21 Madeira Street** (1910) by A.
N. Prentice, is a remarkably convincing piece of
Cotswold Tudor. Surprisingly, there is little Baronial:
though **Mars Hill**, 191 Finnart Street, has its crow-
step gable and bartizan and T. L. Watson's **Birnam**,
88-90 Newark Street, some pedimented dormers and a
scallop-slated ogee tower.

Brisbane Street is strongly walled on each side
by the flat facades of three-storey tenements all with
raised ground floor, front stair and high close-mouth
doorpiece. Stretches of Ardgowan, Finnart, South,
Kelly and Patrick Streets are similar. Some isolated
blocks with turnpike stairs exist but, during the 1870s
and '80s, the majority follow the established Greenock
model. Later blocks, however, are more boldly
modelled with canted bays and generally more
decoratively treated. By far the most splendid of these
is **Sandringham Terrace** (1900-01), 1-12 Esplanade,
and its continuations at **4-10 Margaret Street** and **1
Fox Street**. This four-storey red sandstone terrace
undulates in full-height bowed bays along its
symmetrical esplanade front — the finest *fin-de-siècle*
property in Greenock. Quite unique and valuable are
the dado borders of tiles which line the closes at 4, 8
and 10 Margaret Street and 3 Sandringham Terrace:
manufactured by J. Duncan Ltd. of Glasgow, they
picture the scenes of the Clyde — hills and river,
steamers and yachts.

Top Brisbane Street, c. 1900.
Middle Birnam, 88-90 Newark
Street.
Above Sandringham Terrace.

Rapid expansion in the West End created a need
for churches too. Fortunately the factional proclivities
of Victorian religion were strong in Greenock so that

Above St Andrew's Church.

Inverclyde District Libraries

not only were all nuances of spiritual belief provided for but, in doing so, the townscape was enriched and accented by a variety of church buildings. **St Mark's** 113 **Greenbank** (1862) at the junction of Ardgowan Street and Kelly Street, is an early work of John Honeyman; a high and wide nave church in good First Pointed. In the main gable is a wheel window and, high up in the narrow transept gable, that leaf-shaped Dunblane-derived window which Ruskin had so enthused over in his Edinburgh lectures a decade earlier. John 114 Starforth's more elaborately decorated **St Andrew's Church** (1871), formerly Trinity, on Union Street, also wears this same Dunblane motif, as does **Finnart Church** (1882-83), Madeira Street, a competition winner designed in two weeks by McKissack and Rowan. Though this last has W. G. Rowan's characteristic ventilator *flèche*, there are no spires west of Nelson Street. Starforth's church does, however, have a high balustraded tower — an element reduced to a snecked rubble keep in the rudimentary Gothic of George Goldie's **St Mary's Church** (1862) on 115 Patrick Street. Far from rudimentary is **Finnart St Paul's Church** (1893), Newark Street, where R. Rowand Anderson's superb Perpendicular Gothic mouldings still have the well-kept air of suburban affluence able to afford the best — but, again, no spire! Hippolyte Blanc gets closest with the tall saddleback tower of **Greenbank Church** (1882) at the corner of Kelly Street and Newton Street.

116 **Old West Kirk**
James Miller (rebuilt 1926-28)

Old West Kirk.

Walker

Transferred from its 16th century location at the foot of Nicolson Street to its Seafield site in the 1920s as a result of the post war expansion of Harland and Wolff's shipyard. Negotiations were protracted but, in the end, the church did well. In January 1919, the owners of the threatening yard, wrote

. . . we undertake to present the ground known as Seafield to the church authorities . . . and remove all the existing buildings thereon. To take down the old church and build a replica of it at Seafield with another design of steeple, including extra windows requested, the existing illuminated windows and mural tablets being carefully preserved and transferred to the new church.

The internal woodwork excluding the roof, and other ecclesiastical fittings to be re-used, as far as they are found suitable. We are agreeable to build and present to the church, a parochial hall, to be erected within the grounds of the new site, and finally lay out the grounds.

The **Pirrie Hall** (1922-25) was built first. In squared hammer-dressed rubble with ashlar margins, it was strangely English — high open timber purlin roof, low eaves, leaded Tudor windows. Then came the church, its cruciform plan, walls, tracery and external balustraded stair all re-created. Roofs and tower — again rather English — are new. There is stained glass by Burne-Jones and Rossetti. In the grounds, Miller devised a plot of old table tombs and in the boundary wall, a random display of gravestones from the old kirkyard, some dating from the 17th century.

Besides houses and churches there are few other buildings of note in the West End. Those of 1930s' provenance are certainly the most interesting: a long 117 one- to two-storey brick block at **1 Campbell Street** (1939) and James Miller's dark red brick **Ear, Nose and Throat Hospital** on Eldon Street, changing cleverly from sober neo-Georgian beginnings (1937-39) to the parapetted pavilions and sun rooms of its later extensions (1943). But two other buildings should be mentioned. On Madeira Street, Burnet, Bell and Partners' **Greenock Academy** (1964) steps its long classroom block down to five-storeys from a church-like assembly hall on the hill above. And further west, on Newark Street is the wide two-storeyed spread of **Sir Gabriel Wood's Mariners' Home** (1851-54) designed by D. Mackintosh in collegiate Tudor. Through its small leaded panes *fifty aged and decayed merchant master mariners and merchant seamen* could look out with nostalgia on the Firth. At the gushet of Eldon Street with Newark Street the finial-crested eaves of the old **Toll House** (early 19th century) marks the boundary with Gourock.

Greenock's links *with the sea are many, one of the most romantic that of the pirate William Kidd (c. 1645-1701). According to the* Newgate Calendar *of 1824, Captain Kidd "was born in the town of Greenock and bred to sea". Sailing first as a "legitimate privateer", he turned at length to outright piracy as a more lucrative pursuit. A brief career of five or six years' plunder on the high seas brought adventure and booty, but Kidd was eventually tried for murder and piracy and hanged at London on 24th May 1701.*

Sir Gabriel Wood's Mariners' Home.

RCAHMS

K

General view of Gourock, c. 1875.

RCAHMS

GOUROCK

Murray's Handbook of 1855 describes Gourock as *a long line of white houses which stretch round the margin of the bay*. A little shabbier and not quite so white now, the town still has the relaxed air of a promenade. It has little or no industrial pretension. As early as the middle of last century the ropeworks and walk, constructed in 1777, were moved to Port Glasgow, while long before this the herring trade had died (Gourock claims to have cured the first ever red herring in 1688) so that today it is no longer fishing boats which fill its two bays but yachts and dinghies. In short, this is a town devoted to leisure: an energetic beat across the estuary to Hunter's Quay or Kilcreggan; a stroll down the half-mile long esplanade; or simply a seat on the prom, gazing out across the Firth.

72 Cardwell Road (c. 1890), a slated ogee dome sitting on the curved corner of a three-storey ashlar tenement, marks the boundary with Greenock. Uphill is Gourock's so-called *Garden Suburb* — simple two-storey four-in-a-block roughcast terraces stepping up **Manor Crescent** (1911). Ahead, tenements — some, like **58-70** with good *Art Nouveau* tiles in the closes — continue along Cardwell Road.

91-95 Shore Street (c. 1840) is in lower older scale, much altered but retaining a small central

Inverclyde District Libraries

Municipal Buildings.

Spencer & Soutar

pediment shorn of its apex stack. Gabled with rolled skewputts and heavily quoined, the **Victoria Bar**, 105 Shore Street, dates from the 18th century, as does a fragment of an even finer quoined gable with a carved skewputt left standing on the corner of John Street. The monopitches at **Gourock Health Centre** (1979) and **Shore Street** housing (1977), both by J. G. Quigley and Partners, maintain this lower scale: white-walled and black-boarded, the linking housing blocks are penetrated by pends leading into small courts. Public buildings, too, are modest: the **Gamble Institute** (1874-76), Renaissance with a Roman Doric porch and five arched windows along the first floor; and then, grander but still only two-storeys, Stewart Tough and Alexander's **Municipal Buildings** (1923), a stylistic concoction in red sandstone.

But higher scale is never far away. The **Co-operative Buildings** (1895), a red sandstone ashlar tenement on the corner of Shore Street and John Street (note the *Art Nouveau* sign lettering) reach four bay-windowed storeys somewhat crudely balustraded at the eaves. But A. N. Paterson's **Royal Bank** (1915), Adelaide Street, formerly the National Bank, with balconies to the third floor flats and a wide sprocketted eaves, only improves with height. Four-storeys, too, yet blandly horizontal, the curved front of the **Bay Hotel** (1938), by Laird and Napier, sits right at the centre of town, a run-down reminder of '30s' holidays.

St John's Church
J., J. M. and W. H. Hay (1857)
A Disruption kirk rubble-built in mid Decorated Gothic taking advantage of its elevated site above Kempock Point. Bruce and Sturrock raised a crown spire (1877-78) over the Hays' diagonally buttressed tower base. In fact, almost all Gourock's churches — certainly the better ones — are situated on the higher ground above the shore road.

Spencer & Soutar

St John's Church.

Top Old Gourock Parish Church.
Above Granny Kempock.

Below 46 Kempock Street.
Right Gourock Central Senior
School.

St Ninian's Church (1879-80), Royal Street, is Early English in style, flatted to accommodate a schoolroom below. It has been airily enlarged in 1983 by J. G. Quigley with leaded glass gablet bays and just a hint of Mackintosh. Farther south along Royal Street is the **Old Gourock Parish Church** (1832-33; enlarged 1882, 1900), perhaps by James Dempster, its castellated facade fronted by a bartizaned battlemented tower aligned on the short steep tree-lined hill of Church Street. Most picturesque is **St Bartholomew's Church** (1857) which overlooks West Bay from Barrhill Road. A small Decorated nave and chancel; rather English in disposition, it is nonetheless Scottish Episcopal in denomination, the work of local architect J. C. Sharp.

For Mackintosh devotees **Gourock Central Senior School** (1908), Binnie Street, by A. Cullen, deserves a look. A composition of two semi-circular glazed staircase towers, each with its half cone slated roof, its design is based patently if heavy-handedly on Mackintosh's Scotland Street School in Glasgow (1904-06). And for the superstitious there is **Granny Kempock**, an ancient monolith worn to almost human configuration, now tucked away behind Castle Gardens; for fishermen and sailors setting out on a long voyage or bride and groom setting out on a life together, seven times round the stone would, it was said, ensure good fortune.

Kempock Street bends abruptly west to continue the shore route down a busy shopping street. A run of early 19th century buildings barely manages to hold a consistent eaves along the landward side of the street. Opposite, there is no such discipline; **46 Kempock Street** (1884), however, is a distinguished gable-fronted tenement with two bulbous oriels massively corbelled from first floor. Tantalising views of the estuary are glimpsed on this seaward side until at the open-air **Swimming Pool** (1909; reconstructed 1969),

Cragburn Pavilion.

the Esplanade proper begins along Albert Road. **Craigbank** (1905), a long untidily elevated tenement terrace at 59-91 Albert Road, intervenes to reaffirm a sense of enclosure, but otherwise the rest of Gourock is given over to the Clyde.

Along the front the houses are generally late Georgian, none comparable with the West End mansions of Greenock and many inelegantly altered. But there are good things too. **16 Albert Road** is pavilion-roofed with consoled windows and a porch of Ionic columns; **76-78** is similar with pilaster quoins; **84** has a well detailed Greek Doric porch, not pedimented but with a good entablature; at **114-15** the doorpiece is Roman Doric, projecting from a wider pilastered opening. More four-storeyed tenements interrupt the sequence: **Maybank**, 94 Albert Road, much enriched by mouldings, string coursing and stub column margins to the top floor windows; **Ashburn Gate** and **Ashburn Gardens** (1911-13) in red sandstone ashlar with elaborately Mannerist close entries. Aberrant, too, is J. & J. A. Carrick's **Cragburn Pavilion** (1935-36), now a bleak auditorium box in brick and stucco but retaining some Art Deco fluting. **Queen's Hotel**, a mid 19th century house, looks uneasily compressed in a tenement *cul-de-sac*. **Ivybank** at 17-18 Ashton Road is late Georgian, still with space to breathe — and a fully developed Greek Doric porch. Somewhat earlier, **Whitebank**, 43 Ashton Road, is a high two-storey-and-attic villa with skew gables curving over windowed quadrant corners. Rather later are **48 Ashton Road**, a cottage villa whose bell-casted roof projects over bay windows and columned verandah porch, and **Kelvington**, 49-50 Ashton Road, a tall two storeys with narrow columned

Whitebank, Ashton Road.

141

Above right Castle Levan Hotel.
Above Castle Levan.

mullions to all its bays and bows. Thereafter, along Cloch Road between-the-wars bungalows are the rule until **Castle Levan Hotel**, a large but dull early 19th century house, and some even duller flats and houses of recent date looking far from worthy of the prospect they enjoy.

Castle Levan

(From 14th century)

An L-plan structure now restored and reconstructed as a home. Perched on the edge of a deep gorge, the old tower house rises through the trees to a wallhead of massive alternate corbelling from which emerge the crow stepped gables of a new dormered caphouse.

Back along the hillside, enjoying views over the Firth, are many more houses of less ancient date. Best from the 19th century is **Glenacre** (c. 1870), 16-18 Victoria Road, a pavilion-roofed mansion with tripartite windows, a bracketted eaves and exuberantly decorated with strapwork and incised neo-Grec ornament. On Trumpethill the four copper-roofed glazed pavilions of **Shambala** (1968), designed by Tony Cicalese of the Boys Jarvis Partnership, show what 20th century design can do given a rich client, a magnificent site and good architects.

Shambala, Trumpethill.

Walker

INVERKIP
Cloch Lighthouse
(1795-97)

Cloch Lighthouse.

Out of sight *of Gourock, the Cloch was not, however, out of earshot and when a fog-horn came into operation in 1897, there were many, not only in Gourock but across the water in Dunoon too, who complained bitterly. A heated correspondence ensued in the press during which a rather more charitable writer rebuked his neighbours with a reminder that "A fog-horn is not a musical instrument, and were it so it never would be where it is. That the sound is not that of angelic harps may be admitted, but there is at least as much melody in it as in an average Wagnerian opera."*

Despite its expansion west, Gourock does not reach Cloch Point. Consequently, when the A78 takes a sudden swing south, the thick white lighthouse stack is abruptly revealed as a single architectonic accent rising out of the coastal landscape. Designed by Glasgow architect James Clarkson and Edinburgh engineers Thomas Smith and Robert Stevenson, the tower rises some 80 feet to a wallhead walk above which a domed facetted light (no longer manned since 1973) beams out across the Firth twinning with the Gantocks Light off Dunoon to illuminate the limits of the narrowing channel.

Clustered beneath the lighthouse is a group of slated dwellings including the original keeper's house all somewhat recast with crow-steps and hood mouldings to match the Baronial Gothic of later residential accommodation added by the roadside in the middle of last century.

The construction of the Cloch light led to the building of this coastal road. It is a beautiful route, passing the grassy shore of Lunderston Bay — now part of the Clyde-Muirshiel Country Park — before diverting inland at Ardgowan Estate.

Ardgowan House
Hugh Cairncross (1797-1801)
Built for Sir John Shaw-Stewart, this might fairly claim to be the finest country house in Renfrewshire. It is a large classical mansion, pedimented over four giant order Corinthian pilasters on the east and bow-fronted to the west. Here and there arched forms reverberate across the facades from single round-headed openings to tripartite Venetian windows. Changing the stylistic idiom to Decorated Gothic but continuing the linear layout to the north is the family chapel of **St Michael and All Angels** (1854-56) by John Henderson, and in the grounds a towered stables

Ardgowan House.

Inverclyde District Libraries

Top Inverkip from west.
Middle Woodside Cottage.
Middle Inverkip Parish Church.
Above Langhouse.

block and the roofless ruined keep of **Ardgowan Castle** (late 15th century?).

South, past **Bridgend Cottages**, a cluster of roughcast gable-fronted terraces built for estate workers, is the village of Inverkip. A dual carriageway streaks past while life here seems almost to have returned to that gentler tenor which John Galt drew upon for his *Annals of the Parish.* The houses are generally early 19th century, two-storey, plain and rubble-built: **Burnside House** and the **Old Manse**, on opposite sides of the street, are typical. **Loaf Cottage** adds crow-steps to the formula while **Alexandra Place** boasts scroll club-skews. Higher and grander, **Inverkip Hotel** has a Roman Doric doorpiece. At **Jack Place** and through a pend at **Seaview**, some charming forestairs reveal that what appears to the street as a two-storey house is in fact flatted. More obviously flatted is **Clyde View**, a roughcast tenement with a bizarrely mansarded second floor and attics above. **Kirkbraefoot Cottage** and **Woodside** (c. 1860), at opposite ends of the village, are single-storey; the latter less rustic, having a parapetted eaves on which sit two classical urns transposed from some earlier structure on Ardgowan Estate.

Inverkip Parish Church (1804-05)
Strongly Presbyterian in its T-plan and severe masonry. A belfried pediment with a clock in the tympanum surmounts the projecting arm of the T. Uphill, behind the manse, at the site of an earlier kirk, is the old graveyard with several 18th century stones and the Gothic Revival tomb of Dr James *Paraffin* Young (1811-83), pioneer of oil technology, who lived at Kelly, Wemyss Bay. Young's home (built 1793) has gone — as has William Leiper's replacement **Kelly House** (1890), burnt down in 1913, various circumstances, including a report that *two muddy and dishevelled women who boarded a train at Fairlie shortly after the fire had started looked suspiciously like the culprits,* combining to lay the blame on the Suffragettes. A cathartic latter-day echo of Inverkip's 17th century notoriety for witches? An eerie legacy still seems to linger around the tombs and in the dark wooded fissures of Daff Glen, while further on where the road ends, at **Langhouse** (c. 1848), a castellated Gothic confection of turrets wrapped around the nucleus of a 1705 farmhouse, they still boast a ghost!

Round the corner from Inverkip — another exclamation mark in the landscape! Another Cloch, but more emphatic, more dramatic, the high concrete flue of **Inverkip Power Station** soars out of two immense glazed cages set on a blank black plinth. Intrusive yes, but magnificent too.

RCAHMS

Castle Wemyss illustrated in Millar's *Castles & Mansions of Renfrewshire*, 1889.

WEMYSS BAY

A watering-place of modern origin, says one 19th century guidebook. It was, and has remained, very much the consequence of the rail connection to Glasgow (1865) and the regular steamer service to Rothesay (1870). Sailings on the Firth have, of course, greatly diminished and Glaswegians seek holidays further afield; even so, Wemyss Bay expands, albeit as little more than a dormitory settlement.

Past **1-6 Forbes Place** (c. 1850), a symmetrical gabled terrace with hood mouldings and decoratively bargeboarded porches, and beyond Pugin and Pugin's small neo-Perpendicular **St Joseph's Church** (1900-01) — both carried out in the local red sandstone — a turn right at the turretted estate lodge-houses reveals some earlier houses of interest. **Dunloe** is the result of two phases of buildig: first a Baronialised mansion (1862) occupying part of the site of four late 18th century houses once known as *New Glasgow*, it was thoroughly remodelled in 1889 and 1894 by John Honeyman, becoming more massively and decoratively Scottish. Perched on the escarpment is **The Cliff** (1874-84), also by Honeyman, a vast Culzean-inspired pile in local stone, surrounded by various ancillary offices, including a coachman's house (1901), by John Fairweather, in similar style. Nestling beneath, on Undercliff Road, is J. T. Rochead's **Ferncliff** (c. 1860), a jaggedly garnished Gothic villa deteriorating rapidly. John Burnet's episcopal **Inverclyde Church** (1879) has already gone as has James Salmon's **Wemyss House**. But the greatest loss is undoubtedly **Castle Wemyss**. Purchased in 1860

Ferncliff.

RCAHMS

Wemyss Bay Station from the south.

by John Burns, owner of the Cunard Line and later Lord Inverclyde, the house was completely rebuilt in the hard-edged Baronial of Robert Billings. Spectacularly sited on the cliff with superb views west, the castle he created was a rambling affair with a *wild, serrate skyline*: a genuinely romantic conceit. The American General Sherman, the explorer Stanley, the novelist Trollope, the Emperor Haile Selassie, were all guests here. Those who come now find a solitary flagpole and a mountain of soft rust-red sandstone rubble heaped amid the rhododendrons.

If Castle Wemyss is a disappointment, **Wemyss Bay Station** (1903-04) is an astonishing delight. There are several buildings, all designed by the prolific James Miller for the Caledonian Railway: a house and cottages on the main coast road and the station building itself, are built in half-timbered, red-tiled, turn-of-the-century Tudor using local red stone for plinths and dressings. A striped clocktower catches the eye from ship or shore. But it is inside that catches the imagination. Everything is roofed in a bright, light, fully-glazed lattice steel structure which curves fluently not only in section but in plan too. Around the central semi-circular booking office shallow-arched canopies slide out like sinuous octopus tentacles over arcaded platforms and down the ramped hall leading to the pier and the Rothesay ferry. It is a miracle of intersecting curves: the finest railway architecture in Scotland.

Wemyss Bay Station interior.

ACKNOWLEDGEMENTS

Many people have helped in the compilation of this book. Charles McKean and David Walker have both read the text and I am particularly grateful for their suggestions and criticisms. I also wish to record my thanks to Catherine Cruft, Ian Gow and the staff at the Royal Commission on the Ancient and Historical Monuments of Scotland, James Mackie and Neil Pirrit of Inverclyde District Council Planning Department, Joy Monteith at the Central Library, Greenock, Lesley Couperwhite at the Watt Memorial Library, Greenock, John Dunbar of Renfrew District Council Planning Department, Ken Hinshalwood, Local Historian at the Central Library, Paisley, Robert Saunders at Paisley Museum; to Peter Robinson, Pamela Robertson and Fiona Sinclair; to the Department of Architecture and Building Science at the University of Strathclyde who have indulged my attenuated activity on this guide and whose students' work in the field of historical research continuously adds to my knowledge; to all those architects who have readily responded to my enquiries; and to those many owners of properties who have so hospitably reacted to my disturbing their privacy.

Though the guide attempts to be comprehensive, it cannot hope to be all-inclusive. For omissions which may irritate the reader I can only apologise. I do the same for any errors.

Special thanks is due to Ellen Craig for typing — and re-typing — my manuscripts.

WORKS CONSULTED FOR THIS GUIDE

A guide such as this permits only the briefest referencing of sources. Numerous local records, histories, guidebooks and pamphlets have been consulted but it would be needlessly pedantic to list these here. Several more significant sources — both general and particular — should, however, be mentioned. These are:

Billings, R. W., *The Baronial and Ecclesiastical Antiquities of Scotland*, 1852; Butt, J., *The Industrial Archaeology of Scotland*, 1967; Crawfurd, A., *Cairn of Lochwinyoch Matters*, 1827-54; Crawfurd, G., *A General Description of the Shire of Renfrew*, 1710 (1818); Forsyth, R., *The Beauties of Scotland*, 1806; Groome, F. H., *Ordnance Gazeteer of Scotland*, 1882-85; Hay, G., *The Architecture of Scottish Post-Reformation Churches*, 1957; Heron, R., *Scotland Delineated*, 1799; Hume, J. R., *The Industrial Archaeology of Scotland*, 1976; McDonald, H., *Rambles Round Glasgow*, 1854; MacGibbon, D. and Ross, T., *The Castellated and Domestic Architecture of Scotland*, 1887-92; Marwick, J. D., *The River Clyde and its Burghs*, 1909; Millar, A. H., *The Castles and Mansions of Renfrewshire and Buteshire*, 1889; Metcalfe, W. M., *A History of the County of Renfrew*, 1905; Metcalfe, W. M., *A History of Paisley, 600-1908*, 1909; Ramsay, P. A., *Views in Renfrewshire*, 1839; Semple, W., *The History of the Town and Parish of Paisley*, 1782; Smith, R. M., *The History of Greenock*, 1921; Smout, T. C., *A History of the Scottish People*, 1971; *The Statistical Accounts for Renfrewshire*; Taylor, C., *The Levern Delineated*, 1831; Wilson, J., *General View of the Agriculture of Renfrewshire*, 1812; *The Old Country Houses of the Old Glasgow Gentry*, 1878.

Photographs: The source of each photograph is credited alongside. Particular thanks, however, is due to the RCAHMS.

The support of Inverclyde District Council in the production of this guide is gratefully acknowledged.

Front cover: Newark Castle and the Clyde Estuary by Sam Bough (courtesy Christie's).
Design: Dorothy Steedman.

Maps: The maps were drawn by Frank Walker based upon the outline of Malcolm V. Nicolson's Street Guides, to whom we are indebted.

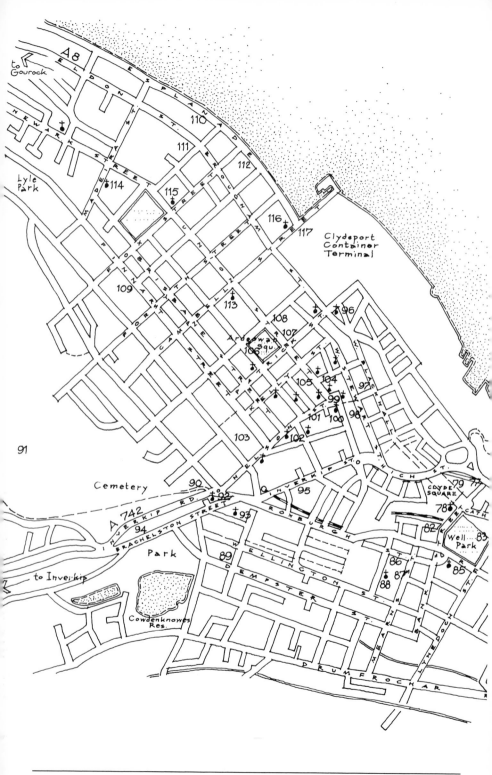

to Gourock

△8

ESPLANADE

NEWARK

Lyle
Park

110

111

112

114

115

116

117

Clydeport
Container
Terminal

109

113

108

107

106

Ardgowan
Squ.

96

105

104

99

97

98

101

100

103

102

91

Cemetery

90

92

A742

INVERKIP RD

BRACHELSTON STREET

94

95

93

to Inverkip

Park

89

Cowdenknowes
Res.

WELLINGTON

DEMPSTER ST.

ROXBURGH

86

87

88

CLYDE
SQUARE

79

78

82

Well
Park

83

85

DRUMFROCHAR

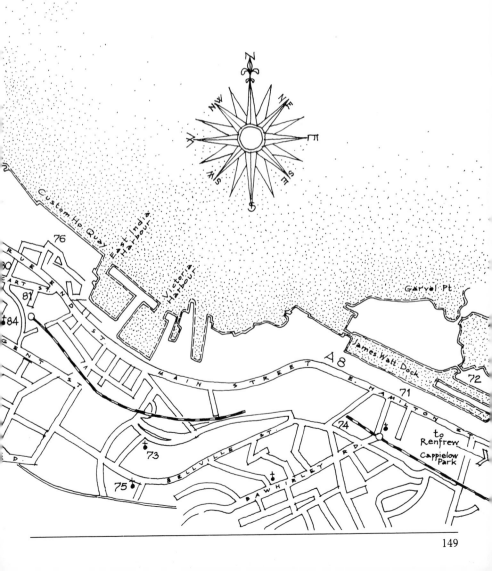

N
NW · NE
W · E
SW · SE
S

Custom Ho Quay

East India Harbour

Victoria Harbour

Garvel Pt

76

80

81

84

James Watt Dock

Δ8

71

72

MAIN STREET

E. HAMILTON ST

73

74

75

BELLVILLE ST

DAWHIRLEY RD

to Renfrew

Cappielow Park